KU-167-439

To [illegible]

Hope you enjoy many of these meals together

Carol Cameron.

THE BUSY COOK'S
COOKBOOK

THE BUSY COOK'S COOKBOOK

JUSTINE DRAKE

PHOTOGRAPHY BY
ROGER BELL, MARTIN GENT, FRANZ LAUINGER, JOHAN PIETERSE

First published in the UK in 1994 by
New Holland (Publishers) Ltd
37 Connaught Street
London
W2 2AZ

Copyright © 1994 New Holland (Publishers) Ltd

All rights reserved. No part of this publication may be reproduced, stored
in a retrieval system or transmitted, in any form or by any means,
electronic, mechanical photocopying, recording or otherwise, without the prior
written permission of the copyright owners and publishers.

ISBN 1 85368 305 1

Editor: Tessa Kennedy
Editorial assistant: Glynne Williamson
Designer: Janice Evans
Assistant designers: Lauren Mendelson and Lellyn Creamer
Photographers: Roger Bell, Martin Gent, Franz Lauinger, Johan Pieterse

Typesetting by Ace Filmsetting Ltd, Frome, Somerset
Reproduction by Unifoto (Pty) Ltd
Printed and bound in Singapore by Tien Wah Press (Pte) Ltd

CONTENTS

INTRODUCTION

Food is one of the great pleasures of life and this cookbook is being published at a time when more of us are choosing to entertain and eat at home.

Good cooking is an art, but most important, a means of giving and sharing pleasure. Nineties people are so busy that there is less time to shop and to spend in the kitchen. This book will enable its readers to produce delicious dishes, from classic soups to gourmet pastas, that look as good as they taste. And the secret ingredient is that the recipes show you how to do it all quickly, effortlessly and, above all, stylishly.

I hope that this easy and imaginative guide to good food in the Nineties will become your constant companion and bring you, and those who share your meals, good times together.

Liz Butler

ITALIAN-STYLE TOMATO SOUP

butter and olive oil for frying
2 onions, chopped
2 carrots, grated
3 stalks celery, chopped
1½ chicken stock cubes
750 ml (1¼ pints) water
2 x 400 g (14 oz) cans tomatoes, diced, juice retained
100 g (3½ oz) canned tomato purée
5 ml (1 tsp) sugar
salt and milled pepper
6 fat cloves garlic, crushed
10 basil leaves, chopped
SERVES 4

Heat butter and oil, add onion, carrot and celery. Sauté for 5 minutes. Dissolve stock cubes in water. Add remaining ingredients, except garlic and basil. Bring to the boil, then reduce heat and simmer for about 1 hour. (At this stage, soup may be puréed as shown in the photograph, but this is not necessary and it's easier, nicer, left chunky.) Five minutes before serving, season to taste, add garlic and basil. Serve with crusty bread and grated Parmesan cheese.

COOK'S NOTES

▲ It is important to add the basil and garlic at the last minute, as their flavour is otherwise lost during the lengthy cooking process.
▲ Any leftover soup may be frozen for later use.

GREEN SUMMER SOUP

15 g (½ oz) butter
1 bunch spring onions
2.5 ml (½ tsp) dill seed (optional)
large iceberg lettuce, shredded
8 large courgettes, grated
45 ml (3 tbsp) chopped parsley
750 ml (1¼ pints) chicken or vegetable stock
salt and milled pepper
45 ml (3 tbsp) chopped basil leaves
about 125 ml (4 fl oz) single cream
SERVES 4

Melt butter in a large saucepan. Add onions and sauté for a few minutes. Add dill and stir to coat. Add lettuce, courgettes and parsley and sauté for a few minutes. Increase heat and add stock. Bring to the boil, then reduce heat and simmer for 8 – 10 minutes. Purée until smooth. Season to taste, stir in basil leaves and add cream. Remove from heat and chill. Serve well chilled, with a sprinkling of chopped fresh herbs.

COOK'S NOTES

▲ Save time by using 2 chicken or vegetable stock cubes to make the stock.
▲ Cut calories by using fromage frais or yoghurt instead of cream.
▲ Spinach, patty pan squash, peas, broad beans and asparagus will all make great additions to the soup.

CHUNKY HADDOCK CHOWDER

Our hassle-free version of the all-American chowder is delicious

sunflower oil and butter for frying
1 large onion, finely chopped
3 large potatoes, peeled and diced
about 600 ml (1 pint) chicken stock
425 g (15 oz) canned creamstyle sweetcorn
400 g (14 oz) canned whole kernel corn
about 400 g (14 oz) haddock, lightly steamed
salt and milled pepper
chopped chives
SERVES 4

Heat oil and butter in a large saucepan and sauté onion and potato for about 4 minutes. Add chicken stock, bring to the boil, reduce heat, cover and simmer until soft, about 20 minutes. Add both varieties of corn and continue cooking for about 5 minutes. Roughly flake steamed haddock and gently stir into chowder. Season to taste. Cook for a further 2 – 3 minutes and serve garnished with chopped chives.

COOK'S NOTES

▲ Vegetable or fish stock may be used instead of chicken stock.
▲ These days, canned salmon is comparatively expensive, but it is a wonderful substitute for the haddock. Use a 200 g (7 oz) can and garnish chowder with fresh dill. If dill is not available, use parsley.
▲ Either frozen or canned corn may be used.

CHILLED CUCUMBER AND YOGHURT SOUP

Easy, delicious and low on calories. Garnish with nasturtium flowers, if available, or lots of chopped chives

2 cucumbers, chopped and seeded
500 ml (17 fl oz) water
500 ml (17 fl oz) natural yoghurt
10 ml (2 tsp) honey
salt and milled pepper
fresh dill, basil or chives, chopped
SERVES 4

Purée cucumber, water, yoghurt, honey and seasoning together. Stir in your choice of herb – all three may be used if desired. Chill well and serve with rye or wholemeal bread.

COOK'S NOTES

▲ For a slightly different flavour, purée watercress and/or lettuce with the cucumber.
▲ Single cream may be used instead of yoghurt, or half quantities of each, if desired. Weak chicken or vegetable stock may be used instead of the water, but do not then add too much salt as the stock is already seasoned.

CAULIFLOWER SOUP

500 g (18 oz) cauliflower, frozen
 or fresh
375 ml (13 fl oz) chicken stock
500 ml (17 fl oz) milk
salt and milled pepper
150 ml (¼ pint) double cream or
 natural yoghurt
SERVES 4

If using a fresh cauliflower, wash, trim and cut into florets. Bring chicken stock to the boil and cook cauliflower until tender but still crisp. Remove cauliflower with a slotted spoon; set aside. (If using frozen cauliflower, cook until just tender.) Add milk and seasoning. Purée cauliflower in a blender or food processor; add to soup. Stir in cream or yoghurt and heat soup to a gentle simmer. Serve hot.

COOK'S NOTES

▲ Serve topped with a sprinkling of finely grated cheese.

▲ For extra flavour, add a pinch of ground cumin or nutmeg.

QUICK FRENCH ONION SOUP

This soup can be prepared in advance and reheated when needed

4 large onions, sliced
2.5 ml (½ tsp) sugar
30 ml (2 tbsp) sunflower oil
2 x 275 ml (9 fl oz) cans beef consommé
500 ml (17 fl oz) beef stock made with 1 cube
30 ml (2 tbsp) brandy

TOPPING
30 ml (2 tbsp) Gruyère or Cheddar cheese
4 slices French bread
20 ml (4 tsp) chopped parsley
SERVES 4

Sprinkle onions with sugar and fry in heated oil over high heat until lightly browned – watch out for burning. Add consommé, stock and brandy. Bring to the boil and simmer for about 5 minutes. Spoon soup into heated bowls, top with cheese toasts and sprinkle parsley over. Serve immediately.
TOPPING: Sprinkle cheese over bread and grill until bubbling.

CHILLED MINT AND PEA SOUP

250 g (9 oz) frozen petits pois
200 ml (7 fl oz) canned pea soup
750 ml (1¼ pints) chicken stock (made with 2 stock cubes)
about 30 ml (2 tbsp) chopped fresh mint
about 200 ml (7 fl oz) single cream
salt and milled pepper
SERVES 4

Thaw petits pois. Bring canned pea soup and stock to the boil, add petits pois and cook for about 10 minutes. Remove from heat. Add mint and chill. Just before serving, stir in chilled cream and season to taste. To serve, place soup bowls on a bed of crushed ice to keep soup chilled.

COOK'S NOTES

▲ Frozen peas will do just as well as petits pois, but will not be as sweet – add 5 ml (1 tsp) sugar while boiling if you prefer the sweeter flavour.
▲ The soup may be served either hot or cold, and may also be made in advance. Refrigerate until needed and stir in the cream and seasoning just before serving.
▲ Shredded spinach makes a pretty and flavourful alternative to the peas.
▲ Do not use natural yoghurt in place of cream in this soup – it will curdle.

AROMATIC CHINESE NOODLE SOUP

- 5 – 7.5 ml (1 – 1½ tsp) sesame oil
- 1 bunch spring onions, diagonally sliced into 1 cm (⅜ inch) thick slices
- 2 – 3 medium courgettes, diagonally sliced
- 3 x 125 g (4 oz) packets Oriental chicken noodle soup.
- 20 – 30 ml (4 – 6 tsp) soy sauce
- 20 ml (4 tsp) sesame seeds, toasted (optional)

SERVES 4

Heat oil in a saucepan large enough to hold the soup. Add spring onions and courgettes (a mixture of green and yellow courgettes is prettiest). Stir-fry for 1 minute. Add water as directed on soup packet instructions. Bring to the boil. Add noodles and soy sauce and cook until ready, about 3 minutes. Ladle into individual bowls, sprinkle with sesame seeds and serve immediately.

COOK'S NOTES

▲ Sesame oil is quite expensive but it's worth buying as only a tiny quantity is needed and it keeps well.

▲ Shredded chicken and your choice of vegetable may be added.

COURGETTE AND BACON SOUP

This soup takes about 40 minutes to make, but needs very little attention, leaving you free for other tasks – or to relax

- 1 large onion, finely chopped
- 60 g (2 oz) butter or margarine
- 2 potatoes, cubed
- 200 g (7 oz) courgettes, cubed
- 2 chicken or vegetable stock cubes
- 1 litre (1¾ pints) boiling water
- 125 ml (4 fl oz) single cream or natural yoghurt
- 8 rashers rindless back bacon, grilled
- chopped chives or parsley

SERVES 4

Sauté onion in butter until soft and glossy, but not brown. Add potatoes and courgettes and toss in butter or margarine. Dissolve stock cubes in water and add to vegetables. Cover saucepan and bring to boil. Reduce heat and simmer for about 30 minutes. Purée vegetables, return to hob, add cream and heat. Ladle soup into heated bowls, crumble bacon soup into heated bowls, crumble bacon over each serving and sprinkle with herbs. (This soup can be served hot or cold.)

COOK'S NOTES

▲ Vegetarians can omit the bacon and use herbs only.

▲ The soup (without bacon and herb topping) can be frozen and used when needed. Thaw and reheat slowly.

SPINACH AND RAVIOLI BROTH

about 24 ravioli filled with spinach and ricotta
sunflower oil for frying
1 large onion or 1 bunch spring onions, finely chopped
1.5 litres (2¾ pints) chicken stock made with 2½ chicken or vegetable stock cubes
60 ml (4 tbsp) white wine
3.75 ml (¾ tsp) sugar
salt and milled pepper
250 g (9 oz) spinach, shredded
20 g (¾ oz) parsley, chopped
30 – 45 g (1 – 1½ oz) chopped fresh basil, if available
freshly grated Parmesan cheese
SERVES 4

Cook ravioli according to manufacturer's instructions, but cook for 2 – 3 minutes less. Drain, toss in a little oil and set aside. Heat oil in a large saucepan and sauté onion until glossy. Add stock, wine, sugar and seasoning. Bring to the boil, add spinach and parsley and cook for about 5 minutes. Add ravioli and cook for a further 2 – 3 minutes. Remove from heat, stir in basil and serve with grated Parmesan cheese and crusty bread.

COOK'S NOTES

▲ If you need more liquid, increase the water by 250 ml (8 fl oz) and use an extra ½ stock cube.

SIMPLE MINESTRONE

A wonderful soup, to which you can add any leftover vegetables, chicken or sausage that may be lurking in the refrigerator

butter and sunflower oil for frying
3 leeks, sliced
3 cloves garlic, crushed
½ bunch celery, with leaves, chopped
2 large carrots, sliced
400 g (14 oz) canned tomatoes, chopped, juice retained
1.25 litres (2¼ pints) chicken stock, made with 2 cubes
45 ml (3 tbsp) white wine
5 ml (1 tsp) sugar
150 g (5 oz) noodles of your choice
2 x 400 g (14 oz) cans butter, pinto or kidney beans, drained
salt and milled pepper
about 45 ml (3 tbsp) chopped parsley
SERVES 4

Heat butter and oil. Sauté leeks, garlic, celery and carrots for 3 – 4 minutes. Add tomatoes and juice, stock, wine and sugar and bring to the boil. Add noodles and cook according to packet instructions. About 5 minutes before end of cooking time, stir in beans. Season to taste, then sprinkle with parsley. Serve with crusty bread and grated Parmesan cheese.

ORANGE-SCENTED BUTTERNUT SQUASH SOUP

An unusual winter warmer that will soon become a favourite

45 g (1½ oz) butter
1 large onion, chopped
2 medium potatoes, diced
about 750 g (1¾ lb) butternut, peeled, seeded and diced
rind of ½ orange
750 ml (1¼ pints) chicken or vegetable stock, made with 2 cubes
60 ml (4 tbsp) orange juice
pinch ground cinnamon
about 125 ml (4 fl oz) milk
125 ml (4 fl oz) single cream
salt and milled pepper
parsley and strips of orange rind to garnish
SERVES 4 – 6

Melt butter and sauté onion for about 1 minute. Add vegetables, orange rind, stock and orange juice and bring to the boil. Reduce heat, cover and simmer for about 30 minutes, or until vegetables are soft. Sieve or purée soup. Return to saucepan, add cinnamon, milk, cream and seasoning. Slowly bring to the boil, reduce heat and simmer until heated through, a few minutes. Add a swirl of cream to each dish, if desired, and garnish with parsley and orange rind.

COOL BEETROOT SOUP

Elegant and easy to make

675 g (1½ lb) cooked beetroot, shredded
2 chicken stock cubes
450 ml (¾ pint) boiling water
5 – 7.5 ml (1 – 1½ tsp) sugar
salt and milled pepper
250 ml (8 fl oz) soured cream
SERVES 4

Place beetroot, stock cubes, water and sugar in a blender and purée until just smooth. Transfer to a large bowl and season. Stir in most of the soured cream, reserving some for serving. Chill. Before serving, swirl remaining soured cream through, and accompany the soup with boiled baby potatoes or toasted rye bread.

COOK'S NOTES

▲ This soup should not be too acidic – test it after adding the soured cream.

▲ It can also be served hot. After seasoning, heat through and serve with swirls of soured cream.

▲ An even quicker version of this soup can be made using a jar of borscht, available from Kosher sections of large supermarkets.

CLASSIC TOMATO SOUP

Adding cream cheese instead of cream gives a new twist to this winter classic

30 g (1 oz) butter
1 large onion, chopped
1 large carrot, grated
3 cloves garlic, crushed
2 x 400 g (14 oz) cans whole peeled tomatoes, chopped, juice retained
2.5 ml (½ tsp) sugar
salt and milled pepper
1½ chicken or vegetable stock cubes dissolved in 750 ml (1¼ pints) water
15 – 30 ml (1 – 2 tbsp) chopped fresh basil or 5 – 10 ml (1 – 2 tsp) dried
30 – 45 g (1 – 1½ oz) cream cheese
SERVES 4

Heat butter in a large saucepan. Add onion, carrot and garlic and sauté until softened, about 5 – 7 minutes. Add tomatoes (with juice), sugar, seasoning, stock and basil. Stir in cream cheese. Heat through and serve hot with crusty bread.

COOK'S NOTES

▲ For a smoother finish, purée soup before adding the cheese.

▲ This soup is ideal for making in large batches and freezing for later use. Freeze before adding the cheese.

▲ Fresh tomatoes may be used instead of canned, but you'll probably have to add a few tablespoons of canned tomato purée for a more intense flavour.

▲ Double cream may be used instead of the cream cheese.

SPINACH AND POTATO SOUP

This is a fairly thick soup. If you'd like it thinner, add more stock

- 15 g (½ oz) butter or 15 ml (1 tbsp) oil
- 1 large or 2 medium onions, chopped
- 3 large potatoes, peeled and cubed
- 4 – 5 bunches spinach, washed, stalks removed
- 10 ml (2 tsp) lemon juice
- 750 ml (1¼ pints) vegetable or chicken stock, made with 1½ cubes
- 125 – 250 ml (4 – 8 fl oz) single cream
- salt, milled pepper and grated nutmeg to taste
- chopped olives to garnish

SERVES 4

Heat butter or oil in a large saucepan, add onions and sauté until glossy. Add diced potatoes and toss to coat with butter. Coarsely chop spinach and add to onions and potatoes, with lemon juice. Sauté for a few minutes, add stock and bring to the boil. Reduce heat and simmer for about 30 minutes. Mash or purée vegetables, return to heat, bring to the boil. Stir in cream and season. Heat through and serve with wholemeal bread. This soup is equally delicious served cold. Garnish with chopped olives.

COOK'S NOTES

▲ Leeks may be used instead of onions.

▲ Weight watchers may use ½ cream and ½ natural yoghurt. Alternatively, substitute yoghurt for cream; the flavour will be quite different, though.

▲ If you can find it, use fresh baby spinach as it is sweeter and less tough.

ROMAN EGG SOUP

This classic Italian soup, known as *stracciatella*, is absolutely delicious and takes only minutes to prepare

4 eggs
1.25 ml (¼ tsp) lemon juice
60 g (2 oz) freshly grated
  Parmesan cheese
pinch grated nutmeg
pinch salt
1 litre (1¾ pints) chicken stock
15 ml (1 tbsp) chopped parsley
SERVES 4 – 6

Beat eggs, lemon juice, Parmesan cheese, nutmeg and salt together. Add about 125 ml (4 fl oz) chicken stock and the parsley. Set aside. Bring remaining stock to the boil. Pour in egg mixture and stir with a metal whisk for about 2 minutes. Serve hot with bread or toast.

COOK'S NOTES

▲ Using fresh, as opposed to prepacked, Parmesan is essential. A cheaper but equally delicious alternative is freshly grated Pecorino cheese.

▲ Homemade chicken stock is ideal but not everyone has time to make it. If you are using a chicken choose a brand with gentle flavour, which is better suited to this dish.

CURRIED SWEET POTATO SOUP

This delicious soup is, perfect for autumn's cooler weather, and may be made in advance and refrigerated or frozen until needed. To serve thaw (if necessary), reheat slowly over low heat

- 15 g (½ oz) butter
- 1 large onion, finely chopped
- 10 – 15 ml (2 – 3 tsp) medium-strength curry powder
- 3.75 ml (¾ tsp) ground cumin
- 1.25 ml (¼ tsp) ground cinnamon
- 5 ml (1 tsp) ground coriander
- 5 ml (1 tsp) turmeric
- 15 ml (1 tbsp) mango chutney
- 2 – 3 large sweet potatoes, finely chopped
- 1.5 litres (2¾ pints) chicken or vegetable stock, made with 2 cubes
- salt
- 125 ml (4 fl oz) single cream or natural yoghurt (optional)
- fresh coriander to garnish (optional)

SERVES 4

Heat butter in a large saucepan and sauté onion until soft. Add curry powder and spices. Cook, stirring often, for about 2 – 3 minutes. Add chutney and potatoes and toss to coat with spices. Pour in stock and bring to the boil. Reduce heat and cook until potatoes are soft. Leave, covered, until cool. Purée until smooth. Return to hob and heat through. Stir in cream or yoghurt, garnish with fresh coriander and serve the soup with bread or poppadums.

COOK'S NOTES

▲ For more bulk and extra sweetness, add pumpkin at the same time as you add the sweet potatoes.

▲ For an even quicker soup, use already cooked sweet potato.

▲ When buying spices like the ones in this recipe, bear in mind that they lose flavour over time so buy small quantities and replenish every 3 months or so.

▲ Warm, fresh rotis or other Indian breads served with this soup transform it into a filling winter meal.

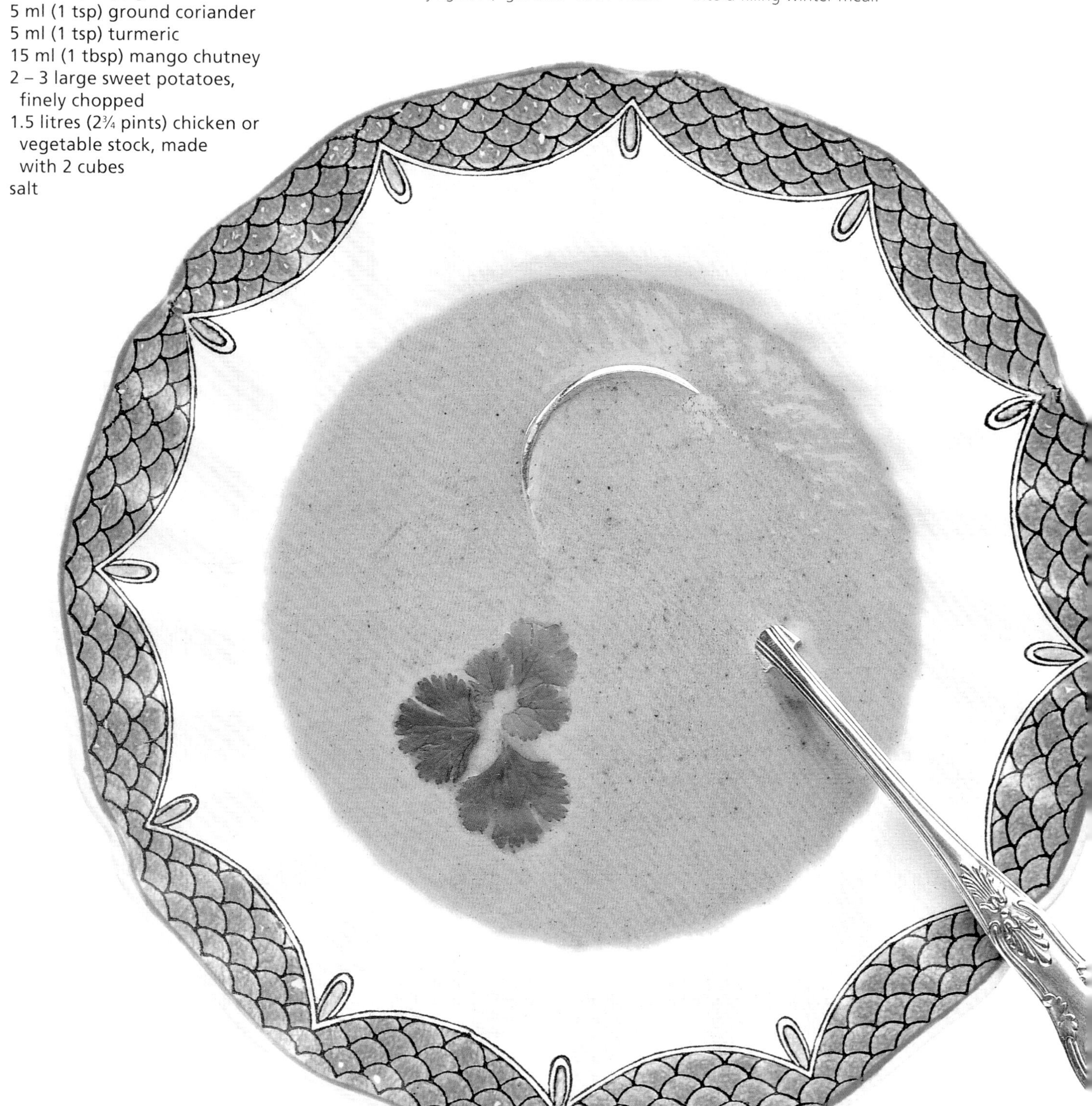

MEDITERRANEAN BEAN SALAD

425 g (15 oz) canned red kidney beans
400 g (14 oz) canned butter beans
400 g (14 oz) canned borlotti or pinto beans
1 large onion, finely chopped
30 ml (2 tbsp) capers
4 – 6 best quality anchovies, chopped or sliced lengthways
juice and rind of 1 small lemon
2 cloves garlic, crushed
75 ml (5 tbsp) olive oil
milled pepper
1 head oak leaf lettuce
3 Little Gem lettuce
SERVES 4

Mix all ingredients, except lettuce, together. If possible, leave to stand for about 1 hour, to allow flavours to develop. Wash and dry lettuce, arrange on a plate, top with bean salad and serve.

COOK'S NOTES

▲ If you don't like anchovies, use water-packed tuna instead.
▲ Serve the bean salad with crusty white bread to mop up the savoury juices.

SPINACH, BACON AND POACHED EGG SALAD

500 g (18 oz) young spinach, shredded (about 2 bunches)
2 small heads chicory
250 g (9 oz) rindless back bacon, chopped
sunflower oil
6 – 8 spring onions
100 g (3½ oz) button mushrooms, sliced
4 eggs
salt, paprika and milled pepper

VINAIGRETTE DRESSING
125 ml (4 fl oz) olive oil
125 ml (4 fl oz) sunflower oil
90 ml (6 tbsp) tarragon vinegar
5 ml (1 tsp) sugar
2.5 – 5 ml (½ – 1 tsp) mustard powder
3 cloves garlic, crushed
salt and milled pepper
SERVES 4

Wash spinach and chicory, dry and chill. Fry bacon in a little oil until crisp. Drain on paper towels. Wash and trim spring onions. Arrange all salad ingredients, including mushrooms and bacon, on 4 plates. Mix dressing ingredients together. Pour a little dressing over salad to coat leaves. Poach eggs in simmering water for 3 – 4 minutes. Drain. Place egg on top of or next to salad, season and serve immediately.

WINTER CAESAR SALAD

sunflower oil for frying
4 slices white bread, crusts removed
assorted salad leaves
300 g (11 oz) green beans, blanched and refreshed
2 avocados, peeled and sliced
3 hard-boiled eggs, quartered
8 – 10 spring onions
60 ml (4 tbsp) freshly grated Parmesan cheese

DRESSING
150 ml (¼ pint) soured cream or Smetena
15 – 30 ml (1 – 2 tbsp) lemon juice
2.5 ml (½ tsp) mustard powder
salt and milled pepper
30 ml (2 tbsp) chopped parsley or dill
SERVES 4

Heat oil in a pan. Cube bread and fry until crisp to make croûtons. Drain on paper towels. Wash salad leaves, dry and arrange on a platter. Layer beans, avocado, egg, spring onion and croûtons on salad leaves. Cover with waxed paper and chill in the refrigerator. Mix dressing ingredients together, drizzle over salad and sprinkle over Parmesan just before serving.

COOK'S NOTES

▲ To boil perfect eggs: place eggs in cold water and bring to the boil. Remove from heat, cover saucepan and stand for exactly 17 minutes. Remove and chill in iced water for 2 – 3 minutes.

CHORIZO SALAD

200 g (7 oz) broccoli, blanched and refreshed
12 – 15 baby potatoes, washed and scrubbed
2 – 3 chorizo or other small spicy sausages
200 g (7 oz) button mushrooms
butter for frying
5 ml (1 tsp) mustard seeds

DRESSING
100 ml (3½ fl oz) sunflower oil
100 ml (3½ fl oz) olive oil
75 ml (5 tbsp) white wine vinegar
2.5 ml (½ tsp) sugar
3 cloves garlic, crushed
salt and milled pepper
SERVES 4

Break blanched broccoli into florets. Boil potatoes in salted water until cooked through, about 15 minutes. Chill and slice thickly. Slice sausage into 1 cm (½ inch) thick slices. Wash mushrooms and dry well. Heat butter, add mustard seeds and sauté until just beginning to pop. Add mushrooms and cook until glossy, brown and cooked through. Mix all salad ingredients together.
DRESSING: Mix ingredients together, chill well and drizzle over salad just before serving.

COOK'S NOTES

▲ Wedges of your favourite salami can replace the chorizo.
▲ Leftover dressing can be stored in a screw-topped bottle in the refrigerator for a few weeks.

CUCUMBER AND NUT SALAD

1 cucumber
250 ml (8 fl oz) natural yoghurt
1 small onion, finely chopped
30 g (1 oz) chopped pecans
or walnuts
salt and milled pepper
snipped fresh dill
SERVES 4

Peel cucumber and halve lengthways. Scoop out seeds using a spoon. Cut crossways into slices. Mix yoghurt, onion, nuts, seasoning and dill. Pour over cucumber and toss lightly until mixed.

COOK'S NOTES

▲ Use parsley instead of dill, if preferred.
▲ Nuts enhance the flavour combination of the cucumber and yoghurt.

AVOCADO AND BACON SALAD

2 medium avocados
lemon juice
salt and milled pepper
250 g (9 oz) lean bacon rashers
assorted lettuce leaved – cos,
butterhead, red oak
2 – 3 hard-boiled eggs
walnut or olive oil
snipped chives
lemon wedges
SERVES 4

Cut avocados in half, carefully peel and remove stones. Dice and sprinkle with lemon juice and seasoning. Cube bacon and fry untill crisp. Drain and set aside. Arrange avocado on a bed of lettuce on individual side plates. Add bacon. Finely chop hard-boiled eggs and sprinkle over top. Drizzle over a little walnut or olive oil or a squeeze of lemon juice. Garnish with snipped chives and lemon wedges.

COOK'S NOTES

▲ The salad ingredients may be tossed together before adding the garnish.
▲ Instead of chopping the hard-boiled eggs, press them through a sieve.
▲ Choose ripe, unblemished avocados to ensure a delicate combination of flavours.

BLUE CHEESE WINTER SALAD

1 large butterhead lettuce
3 courgettes
4 carrots
1 apple or pear
150 g (5 oz) soft blue cheese
100 ml (3½ fl oz) single cream
60 ml (4 tbsp) thick natural yoghurt
2.5 ml (½ tsp) sugar
salt and milled pepper
chives or watercress to garnish
SERVES 4

Tear well-washed lettuce leaves and arrange on a large platter or individual plates. Thinly slice courgettes and carrots into long thin strips or use a potato peeler to make long, soft, paper-thin slices. Thinly slice fruit. Scatter vegetables and fruit over lettuce leaves. Mash cheese and mix with remaining ingredients, except chives, then add extra sugar and seasoning to taste. Spoon a liberal amount into the centre of each salad or, for a large platter, spoon the cheese mixture over in a zig-zag pattern. Top with fresh chives or watercress.

COOK'S NOTES

▲ If you don't like blue cheese, use feta or a mild cream cheese for the dressing.
▲ Weight watchers may use more yoghurt and less cream in the dressing.
▲ Serve the salad as a starter, or with a soup as a main meal.
▲ Prepare the salad just before serving to ensure that the lettuce leaves will be as crisp as possible.

CALIFORNIAN SKATE SALAD

This tart salad was created by Californian chef Wolfgang Puck

assorted lettuce leaves
about 12 baby tomatoes
2 large, fresh skate wings
(750 g – 1 kg/1¾ – 2¼ lb)
flour to coat
olive oil for frying
30 – 45 ml (2 – 3 tbsp) capers
60 ml (4 tbsp) white wine vinegar
salt and milled pepper
pinch sugar
4 sprigs fresh oregano
SERVES 4

Arrange lettuce and tomatoes on 4 individual plates and set aside. Other salad ingredients may be added if desired. Slice skate wings into 2 cm (¾ inch) strips. Dip skate strips into flour and shake to remove excess. Heat olive oil in a large non-stick frying pan. Fry strips, all at once if possible, for about 2 – 3 minutes, turning once. With heat on highest setting, add remaining ingredients except oregano, and toss vigorously. Spoon fish and sauce over each salad. Drizzle with olive oil, garnish with fresh herbs and serve immediately with crusty bread.

COOK'S NOTES

▲ Use olive oil to fry the fish – sunflower oil just doesn't have the right flavour.

AVOCADO, BRESAOLA AND PEAR SALAD

1 large lettuce of your choice
400 g (14 oz) canned broad, kidney or butter beans, drained
3 pears, thinly sliced
2 avocados, sliced into crescents
10 slices bresaola

DRESSING
125 ml (4 fl oz) olive or sunflower oil
60 ml (4 tbsp) wine vinegar
5 ml (1 tsp) sugar
5 ml (1 tsp) mustard powder
5 ml (1 tsp) wholegrain mustard
salt and milled pepper
SERVES 4

Wash lettuce, tear into pieces and arrange on a platter or individual plates. Rinse beans and scatter over lettuce. Arrange pear and avocado slices on top. Grill bresaola for 2 – 3 minutes, or until crisp. (Watch bresaola closely as it cooks very quickly.) Break bresaola into pieces and scatter over salad.
DRESSING: Mix all ingredients together and drizzle over salad.

COOK'S NOTES

▲ Fresh green beans, blanched and refreshed, may be used instead of canned beans, but choose young, slender beans to ensure that they will be tender.
▲ Anchovies or grilled bacon are both good substitutes for the bresaola.
▲ To prevent pears browning while preparing the salad, soak them in a little fresh lemon juice.

ANTIPASTO SALAD

A light lunch or supper dish that keeps well in the refrigerator

425 g (15 oz) canned chickpeas, drained
500 g (18 oz) cooked fusilli (spiral noodles) or noodles
8 cherry tomatoes, quartered
½ cucumber, chopped
1 bunch spring onions, chopped
1 medium red pepper, thinly sliced
60 ml (4 tbsp) chopped parsley
15 ml (1 tbsp) chopped fresh oregano
about 150 – 200 g (5 – 7 oz) feta cheese, crumbled
salt and milled pepper
olive oil
white wine vinegar or balsamic vinegar
SERVES 4 – 6

Mix together all ingredients except seasoning, oil and vinegars. Season well with salt and milled pepper, then drizzle with oil, wine and vinegar. Serve with crusty bread.

COOK'S NOTES

▲ Cut costs by cooking dried chickpeas yourself.
▲ 2 – 3 cloves of crushed garlic give a wonderful flavour.
▲ Other ingredients worth adding are: canned tuna, pilchards or salmon; fresh, cooked or canned whole corn kernels; kidney or butter beans, chopped gherkins, marinated peppers, mushrooms or artichoke hearts.

SUMMER SALAD PLATTER

20 baby potatoes
125 ml (4 fl oz) pesto
60 ml (4 tbsp) single cream
45 ml (3 tbsp) freshly grated Parmesan cheese
salt and milled pepper
250 g (9 oz) green beans
400 g (14 oz) canned butter beans, drained
1 red sweet pepper, sliced into thin strips
1 green sweet pepper, sliced into thin strips
2 cloves garlic, crushed
chopped fresh parsley
juice of ½ lemon
a little olive oil
1 punnet each red and yellow cherry tomatoes
150 g (5 oz) feta cheese, coarsely crumbled
1 bunch spring onions, chopped
a little vinaigrette dressing
assorted lettuce leaves
SERVES 4

Boil potatoes, drain and cool. Mix pesto, cream and Parmesan cheese and season. Pour mixture over still warm potatoes. Set aside. Cook beans in boiling salted water until *al dente*, about 6 minutes. Mix green beans, butter beans and pepper strips together. Toss in crushed garlic, parsley, lemon juice and olive oil and season. Halve tomatoes and toss with feta cheese and spring onions. Drizzle with vinaigrette dressing. Group 3 salads on a platter of lettuce leaves and serve.

MARINATED SQUID AND MUSHROOM SALAD

200 – 300 g (7 – 11 oz) squid rings
175 ml (6 fl oz) water
45 ml (3 tbsp) white wine
8 peppercorns
5 ml (1 tsp) salt
5 ml (1 tsp) sugar
3 garlic cloves, sliced
1.25 ml (¼ tsp) chilli flakes (optional)
250 g (9 oz) button mushrooms
200 g (7 oz)green beans, trimmed
1 large red pepper, sliced
SERVES 4

Wash squid thoroughly and set aside. Bring water, wine, spices, sugar, garlic and chilli to the boil. Add mushrooms and cook for 3 – 5 minutes. Remove, drain and place in salad bowl. Add beans to water and cook for about 8 minutes, until *al dente*, remove, drain and add to mushrooms. Repeat procedure with red pepper strips, cooking for about 2 minutes, and squid, cooking for about 2½ minutes. Toss all ingredients together and, while still warm, pour over a vinaigrette dressing.

COOK'S NOTES

▲ Squid tubes may be used and cut into rings – easier to do while still half frozen than when fully thawed.
▲ Squid gets tougher the longer it is cooked, so be careful.

AUBERGINE, TOMATO AND RICOTTA SALAD

2 small aubergines, sliced
salt
sunflower oil for frying
3 cloves garlic, crushed
3 large ripe tomatoes, sliced
200 g (7 oz) ricotta cheese, sliced
1 large onion, thinly sliced
olive oil
garlic wine vinegar
salt and milled pepper
1 bunch fresh basil or oregano, if available
SERVES 4 – 6

Sprinkle aubergines with salt and allow to stand for about 10 minutes. Heat oil and sauté garlic for about 1 minute. Add aubergines slices and fry on both sides until golden. Remove and drain on paper towels. On a large platter or individual plates, layer tomato, ricotta and aubergines. Scatter onion on top. Drizzle with olive oil and vinegar, season to taste and sprinkle with fresh basil leaves.

COOK'S NOTES

▲ Use only young, slim aubergines – they taste and look better.
▲ Mozzarella cheese can be used instead of ricotta.
▲ Ricotta is not always easy to slice, so if it won't behave, break it into chunks.

RED CABBAGE, POTATO AND BACON SALAD

45 ml (3 tbsp) vinegar
½ small red cabbage, shredded
12 – 16 boiled baby potatoes
about 100 g (3½ oz) green beans, blanched and refreshed
10 rashers rindless back bacon, grilled and chopped
100 g (3½ oz) feta cheese
vinaigrette dressing
SERVES 4

Bring vinegar to the boil, pour over cabbage and toss well. Leave for about 5 minutes, or until softened. Meanwhile, halve baby potatoes and toss with beans and bacon. Mix in softened cabbage and arrange on individual plates or on a platter. Sprinkle with crumbled feta cheese, drizzle with vinaigrette dressing and serve.

COOK'S NOTES

▲ White cabbage may be used instead of red or, if cabbage is not your favourite vegetable, use shredded spinach instead. If you do, omit the vinegar.

TRICOLOUR PASTA SALAD

400 g (14 oz) tri-colour pasta spirals
45 – 60 ml (3 – 4 tbsp) oil
200 g (7 oz) canned water-packed tuna, drained and flaked
10 spring onions, chopped
¼ cucumber, cut into matchsticks
about 12 baby tomatoes, halved
60 ml (4 tbsp) chopped parsley

YOGHURT DRESSING
125 ml (4 fl oz) natural yoghurt
10 ml (2 tsp) white wine vinegar
1 clove garlic, crushed
3. 75 ml (¾ tsp) mustard powder
salt and milled pepper
SERVES 4

Cook pasta according to packet instructions. Rinse with cold water, drain and cool. Toss in oil. Mix tuna, onions, cucumber, tomatoes and parsley together. Gently stir into pasta, making sure all ingredients are well mixed.
DRESSING: Combine all the ingredients, season to taste, and pour over salad.

COOK'S NOTES

▲ Any kind of noodle may be used; the tricolour pasta spirals look attractive.
▲ Canned salmon may be used as an alternative to tuna.
▲ A garlicky vinaigrette dressing is also delicious with this salad.
▲ The pasta may be tossed in butter instead of oil.

CURRIED WHOLEGRAIN SALAD

250 g (9 oz) uncooked brown rice
1 vegetable or chicken stock cube
200 g (7 oz) uncooked brown lentils
15 ml (1 tbsp) sunflower oil
15 ml (1 tbsp) medium-strength curry powder
60 ml (4 tbsp) orange juice
60 ml (4 tbsp) apricot juice
90 g (3 oz) seedless raisins
30 ml (2 tbsp) mango chutney
½ bunch fresh coriander or 5 ml (1 tsp) ground
1 large mango, sliced
flaked almonds, lightly toasted (optional)
SERVES 4

Cook rice with crumbled vegetable or chicken stock cube, according to packet instructions. Rinse with cold water and drain. Cook lentils until just soft, rinse with cold water and drain. Heat oil in a saucepan, add curry powder and cook for 2 – 3 minutes. Add juices, raisins and chutney, and bring to the boil. Reduce heat and simmer for about 5 minutes. Chop coriander and mix gently with rice and lentils. When curry sauce is cool, pour over and mix. Garnish with mango and almonds and serve.

SESAME-COATED CHICKEN LIVERS

Top your favourite salad ingredients with these moist sesame-coated chicken livers

butter and sunflower oil
10 ml (2 tsp) mustard seeds
500 g (18 oz) chicken livers
salt and milled pepper
toasted sesame seeds

DRESSING
200 ml (7 fl oz) olive oil
60 ml (4 tbsp) sherry vinegar or white wine vinegar
15 ml (1 tbsp) wholegrain mustard
2.5 ml (½ tsp) sugar
salt and milled pepper
SERVES 4

Heat butter and oil and add mustard seeds. As seeds begin to pop, add livers. (If livers begin to stick, add extra butter or oil, or a splash of sherry.) Season and cook over high heat for about 3 minutes. Livers should remain pink and moist inside. Remove from pan and roll in sesame seeds while still hot. Set aside and keep hot. Arrange salad ingredients on plates.
DRESSING: Whisk ingredients together.
TO ASSEMBLE: Place warm livers on salad and drizzle dressing over. Serve immediately.

GOAT'S MILK CHEESE SALAD

selection of assorted pretty lettuce leaves, washed
2 – 3 celery stalks, cut into matchsticks
1 bunch watercress

DRESSING
1.25 ml (¼ tsp) mustard powder
30 ml (2 tbsp) each red wine vinegar and white wine vinegar
30 ml (2 tbsp) mango chutney
salt and milled pepper
60 ml (4 tbsp) sunflower oil
60 ml (4 tbsp) olive oil
about 225 g (8 oz) goat's milk cheese
30 ml (2 tbsp) toasted flaked almonds (optional)
SERVES 4

DRESSING: Whisk all ingredients, except cheese and almonds, together. Pour dressing over lettuce, coating each leaf well. Arrange dressed leaves and celery on individual plates or on a large platter. Top with wedges of cheese and sprinkle with almonds. Garnish with watercress and serve immediately with nutty wholemeal bread.

COOK'S NOTES

▲ Feta, mozzarella or blue cheese may also be used.
▲ Instead of almonds, use pine kernels, pecan nuts or walnuts.

PESTO AND SPRING ONION PASTA SALAD

A wonderfully versatile salad that can be served as a main course, side dish or just kept in the refrigerator for random snacking!

500 g (18 oz) farfalle or noodles of your choice
about 45 ml (3 tbsp) homemade or bottled pesto
125 g (4 oz) cream cheese or curd cheese
5 ml (1 tsp) fresh lemon juice
30 – 45 ml (2 – 3 tbsp) grated Parmesan cheese
1 small bunch fresh basil (or preserved in oil)
milk, single cream or natural yoghurt for thinning
6 spring onions, cut into julienne strips
30 ml (2 tbsp) toasted almonds (optional)
SERVES 4

Cook pasta according to packet instructions. Rinse with cold water, drain and cool. Mix pesto, cheese, lemon juice, Parmesan cheese and basil. Pour over pasta and toss lightly to mix. Add a little milk, cream or yoghurt if mixture is too thick. Scatter with spring onions and almonds and serve.

COOK'S NOTES

▲ Strips of red or yellow sweet pepper add colour and crunch.

▲ If bottled pesto is too expensive, finely chop lots of fresh basil and stir into a mixture of cream and yoghurt. Season with salt, milled pepper and freshly grated Parmesan cheese. Add a dash of milk to thin mixture.

SESAME SIRLOIN SALAD WITH CHILLI MAYONNAISE

mixed salad ingredients and fresh herbs of your choice
butter and sunflower oil for frying
400 – 500 g (14 – 18 oz) sirloin steak
milled pepper
5 ml (1 tsp) mustard powder
about 20 ml (4 tsp) toasted sesame seeds (optional)

CHILLI MAYONNAISE
3.75 ml (¾ tsp) crushed chilli
2 cloves garlic, crushed
3.75 ml (¾ tsp) wholegrain mustard
125 ml (4 fl oz) good-quality mayonnaise
60 ml (4 tbsp) thick natural yoghurt
a few drops lemon juice
milled pepper
SERVES 4

CHILLI MAYONNAISE: Mix chilli, garlic, mustard and 5 ml (1 tsp) mayonnaise. Add remaining ingredients. Reserve.

Arrange salad ingredients on 4 plates. Heat butter and oil in a heavy frying pan until almost smoking. Season meat with pepper and mustard and fry to desired degree. Remove from pan and press sesame seeds into top. Slice thickly and arrange on salad. Serve immediately with chilli mayonnaise.

PAPAYA, WATERCRESS AND EMMENTHAL SALAD

1 medium papaya, peeled
16 thin slices Emmenthal cheese
250 g (2 bunches) watercress, washed

DRESSING
125 ml (4 fl oz) olive oil
juice of ½ lemon
2.5 ml (½ tsp) wholegrain mustard
salt and milled pepper
SERVES 4

Halve papaya lengthways, seed and slice into crescents. Arrange papaya, cheese and watercress on a large platter or on individual plates.
DRESSING: Mix ingredients together and pour over salad. Serve with nutty wholemeal bread and butter.

COOK'S NOTES
▲ A sweet melon may be used instead of papaya.
▲ Blue cheese, Port Salut or St Paulin cheeses are good alternatives to the the Emmenthal.

ITALIAN SALAD PLATE

8 slices pepper salami
8 slices mozzarella cheese
12 black or green olives
4 ripe tomatoes, sliced
olive oil
salt and milled pepper
1 bunch fresh basil
SERVES 4

Arrange meat, cheese, olives and tomatoes on individual plates. Drizzle with olive oil, season and scatter fresh basil over. Serve with crusty bread or pitta bread, halved widthways, quartered, brushed with olive oil, seasoned and grilled until crisp, 3 – 5 minutes.
VARIATIONS: Add halved hard-boiled eggs, marinated peppers, mushrooms or mixed vegetables, mortadella, Parma ham, miniature meat balls, ricotta cheese or onion slices to the salad.

COOK'S NOTES
▲ It is imperative that olive, and not sunflower, oil is used.
▲ Chopped sun-dried tomatoes are great with this salad.

SMOKED CHICKEN SALAD WITH HORSERADISH CREAM

1.5 kg smoked chicken
1 large oak leaf or butterhead lettuce, washed
2 curly endive, washed
1 bunch watercress, washed
1 bunch spring onions
1 small papaya, peeled and sliced into crescents
4 baby cucumbers, sliced lengthways

HORSERADISH CREAM
15 – 20 ml (3 – 4 tsp) creamed horseradish
125 ml (4 fl oz) double cream
10 ml (2 tsp) lemon juice
salt and milled pepper
SERVES 4

Carve chicken into suitable salad slices and set aside. Tear lettuce coarsely and use to line a large platter or 4 individual plates. Add endive leaves. Arrange the remaining ingredients, including sliced chicken, as desired.

HORSERADISH CREAM: Mix all ingredients together. Add more horseradish and seasoning as required. Serve separately, drizzled lightly over salad, or place a dollop in centre of salad. Grind black pepper over and serve with wholemeal bread.

COOK'S NOTES

▲ Smoked chicken is available from most delicatessens and large supermarkets. If you prefer, roast chicken may be used.
▲ Bottles or jars of creamed horseradish can be found in most supermarkets.
▲ Use sliced mango instead of papaya.

MUSTARD HAM AND APPLE SALAD

Slices of sweet red apple help to cut the slightly salty flavour of baked ham

- 1 butterhead lettuce, washed and dried
- 8 large slices baked ham
- 8 slices Gruyère or Emmenthal cheese
- 2 red apples, sliced into crescents
- 1 large bunch watercress or rocket, well washed and dried

MUSTARD VINAIGRETTE

- 125 ml (4 fl oz) olive or sunflower oil
- 60 ml (4 tbsp) apple cider or natural vinegar
- 3.75 ml (¾ tsp) mustard powder
- 7.5 ml (1½ tsp) wholegrain mustard
- 5 ml (1 tsp) honey
- salt and milled pepper

SERVES 4

Arrange salad ingredients on a large platter or on individual plates.

MUSTARD VINAIGRETTE: Whisk ingredients together until creamy. Pour dressing over salad just before serving with thick slices of warm crusty bread and butter.

COOK'S NOTES

▲ If Emmenthal or Gruyère is too costly, use mature Cheddar cheese.

▲ Any leftover vinaigrette may be kept in a sealed container for up to 2 weeks.

WARM FETA CHEESE AND POTATO SALAD

Potatoes may be peeled before or after boiling, whichever you find easier

- 4 – 5 large potatoes
- 60 ml (4 tbsp) good quality mayonnaise
- 60 ml (4 tbsp) soured cream or thick natural yoghurt
- 10 ml (2 tsp) white wine vinegar (optional)
- salt and milled pepper
- 7.5 ml (1½ tsp) wholegrain mustard
- 45 ml (3 tbsp) chopped chives
- 45 ml (3 tbsp) chopped spring onions
- 150 g (5 oz) crumbled feta cheese
- optional extras (see Cook's Notes)

SERVES 4 – 6

Boil potatoes until just soft. Drain and peel if necessary. Set aside. Mix remaining ingredients together and adjust seasoning to taste. Chop potatoes into bite-sized cubes. Gently stir cheese mixture and potatoes together. Serve on a bed of crisp lettuce, while still warm.

COOK'S NOTES

▲ Optional extras: chopped hard-boiled egg, chopped gherkins, blue cheese instead of feta, or half of each.

▲ Homemade mayonnaise makes the best and creamiest potato salad.

▲ If making mayonnaise doesn't appeal, use a good quality brand.

COURGETTE AND BACON QUICHE

400 g (14 oz) puff pastry
3 – 4 large courgettes coarsely grated or sliced
200 g (7 oz) rindless back bacon, chopped
250 ml (8 fl oz) single cream or 125 ml (4 fl oz) each natural yoghurt and milk
3 eggs
100 g (3½ oz) grated Cheddar cheese
5 ml (1 tsp) mustard powder
salt and milled pepper
SERVES 4

Preheat oven to 200 °C (400 °F/gas 6). Roll pastry out to fill a greased 25 cm (10 inch) diameter loose-based flan tin. Scatter courgettes and bacon on to pastry base. Beat cream and eggs together, stir in remaining ingredients and pour over base. Bake on second shelf from bottom of oven for 25 minutes. Transfer to middle of oven and bake for 15 minutes, or until pastry is crisp and filling set. Serve with soured cream and chive sauce.

COOK'S NOTES

▲ Either puff or shortcrust pastry may be used for the quiche.
▲ Salami or ham may be used instead of bacon.
▲ To make the soured cream and chive sauce, mix about 125 ml (4 fl oz) soured cream with about 30 ml (2 tbsp) fresh lemon juice, 30 ml (2 tbsp) snipped chives and seasoning to taste.

PARTY PIZZAS

8 medium cheese and tomato uncooked pizzas

TOPPING 1
8 – 12 rashers bacon, chopped
200 g (7 oz) blue cheese, crumbled
8 slices fresh pineapple, cubed
salt and milled pepper

TOPPING 2
3 – 4 small aubergines, cut into 5 mm (¼ inch) thick thick slices
4 – 6 large ripe tomatoes
olive oil
12 cloves garlic, crushed
salt and milled pepper
SERVES 4

TOPPING 1: Layer bacon, cheese and pineapple on to pizza, season to taste and cook according to packet instructions.
TOPPING 2: Sprinkle aubergine slices with salt and allow to stand for at least 1 hour. (NOTE: This is not absolutely necessary if aubergines are young and fresh.) Peel and chop tomatoes and divide between pizzas. Rinse aubergines, dry and brush with olive oil. Spread the aubergines, garlic and seasoning over tomatoes and bake pizzas as directed on packet.

BLUE CHEESE AND SPRING ONION OMELETTE

8 large eggs
40 ml (8 tsp) water
salt and milled pepper
60 – 75 g (2 – 2½ oz) butter
60 g (2 oz) creamy blue cheese
25 ml (5 tsp) curd or cream cheese
single cream or natural yoghurt (optional)
8 spring onions, thinly sliced
salt and milled pepper
SERVES 4

Whisk eggs, water and seasoning together in a large bowl. Heat a large frying pan, preferably nonstick, and melt butter so that it coats entire pan. Just as butter begins to brown slightly (indicating that pan is hot enough), pour in egg mixture. Shake pan to distribute eggs evenly and cook for a few seconds. Mix cheeses together well. If mixture is a little too thick, add a dash of single cream or natural yoghurt. Add spring onions and season. Spoon cheese mixture into centre of omelette. Now comes the art of omelette making – either turn out omelette on to a platter or shake pan vigorously, tilting far edge of pan so that omelette begins to roll over itself. Push any stray egg into omelette with a spatula. Serve with a crisp salad and wholemeal bread.

COOK'S NOTES

▲ Use your favourite cheese (feta is lovely) instead of blue cheese.
▲ For an omelette for one, quarter the ingredients.

FETA AND AVOCADO OMELETTE

A delicious omelette, bursting with flavour and colour. The ingredients should not be doubled as the omelette will end up tough and rubbery; rather make one omelette at a time

3 eggs
20 ml (4 tsp) water
15 ml (1 tbsp) chopped chives
15 ml (1 tbsp) butter
½ small avocado, peeled and diced
30 ml (2 tbsp) crumbled feta cheese
about 12 cherry tomatoes, halved
salted and milled pepper
SERVES 1 – 2

Beat eggs and water together until frothy. Add chives. Heat butter until bubbling. Add egg mixture. Cook, lifting sides frequently to allow egg mixture to run underneath. When cooked around edges but still wet in centre, place avocado, cheese and tomatoes on one half of omelette. Season to taste, flip unfilled side over filling and slide out of pan. Serve immediately with a mixed salad.

TANGY TACOS

8 taco shells

FILLING
butter and sunflower oil for frying
1 large onion, finely chopped
3 cloves garlic, crushed
400 – 500 g (14 – 18 oz) lean beef mince
30 ml (2 tbsp) Worcestershire or soy sauce
1 beef stock cube dissolved in 100 ml
(3½ fl oz) boiling water
30 ml (2 tbsp) white wine
5 ml (1 tsp) sugar
salt and milled pepper
SERVES 4

Preheat oven to 180 °C (350 °F/gas 4). Heat butter and oil in a pan. Add onion and garlic and sauté till soft. Add mince and brown lightly. If pan dries out, add a little stock. Add remaining ingredients, bring to the boil. Reduce heat and simmer until cooked and most moisture has evaporated. Bake taco shells in preheated oven for 5 minutes. Fill with mince filling and serve with a few of these garnishes: shredded lettuce, chopped tomato, onion, celery or gherkins, mashed avocado, grated cheese – just about anything that comes to mind.

COOK'S NOTES
▲ The mince filling can be made in advance and frozen.
▲ Buy taco shells from large supermarkets or delicatessens.

MUSHROOM AND BACON PILAFF

200 g (7 oz) long-grain rice
8 – 10 rashers bacon, chopped
1 onion, finely chopped
½ each red, green and yellow peppers
2 cloves garlic, crushed (optional)
about 100 g (3½ oz) mushrooms, chopped
60 ml (4 tbsp) white wine
15 ml (1 tbsp) soy sauce
salt and milled pepper
SERVES 4 – 6

Cook rice according to packet instructions and set aside. Fry bacon and onion until bacon is just crisp, add peppers and garlic and a dash of oil if necessary. Sauté until just beginning to soften. Add remaining ingredients, including rice, and toss gently to combine flavours. Heat through and serve. A fresh tomato and onion salad with a good vinaigrette dressing makes an ideal accompaniment.

COOK'S NOTES
▲ Leftover pilaff is wonderful served cold as a light lunch dish.
▲ Vegetarians may omit the bacon – it will taste just as good!
▲ Add a little mushroom ketchup to the pilaff to emphasize the flavour, if liked.
▲ To whiten dull, beige-looking mushrooms, soak them in a little fresh lemon juice for a few minutes.
▲ Cooked ham, beef or chicken may be used instead of the bacon.

COCKTAIL PLATTER

1 medium cucumber, peeled
½ small onion, grated (optional)
2.5 ml (½ tsp) salt
250 g (9 oz) smooth cottage cheese
juice of ½ small lemon
2.5 ml (½ tsp) mustard powder
milled pepper
1 large clove garlic, crushed
SERVES 4 – 6

Grate cucumber and onion, place in a sieve to drain, pressing occasionally to remove excess liquid. Meanwhile, blend remaining ingredients together until smooth. Stir in drained vegetables. Season to taste, but do not add extra garlic for at least 30 minutes as it takes a while for the flavour to seep through. If tzatziki is too thick, stir in a little extra yoghurt. Serve with a variety of crisp fresh vegetables, carrot sticks, blanched broccoli and cauliflower florets, mushrooms, cucumber wedges, baby corn, mangetout, blanched beans and red pepper strips.

MAYONNAISE MAGIC
Make an aioli (French garlic mayonnaise) by adding crushed garlic to a good quality mayonnaise, season with milled pepper and lemon juice. Ring the changes with a little tomato paste, a few drops of Tabasco sauce and a little crushed garlic for a tangy pink sauce or, for the green summer look, add a liberal amount of chopped parsley and basil, lemon juice, black pepper and garlic.

SESAME AND GREEN LENTIL DIP

Try this new, delicious and easy party dip!

300 g (11 oz) green lentils, cleaned and soaked
1 vegetable stock cube
1 onion, grated
1 clove garlic, crushed
30 g (1 oz) finely chopped parsley
juice of ½ lemon
45 ml (3 tbsp) sesame seeds, toasted
125 ml (4 fl oz) olive oil
salt and milled pepper
MAKES ABOUT 600 – 750 ML (1 – 1¼ PINTS)

Cook lentils in soaking water with crumbled stock cube until soft. Drain. Place in a food processor with onion, garlic, parsley, lemon juice and sesame seeds and blend until smooth. With motor running, slowly add oil in a thin stream. Season to taste and serve with toasted pitta triangles and crudités.

COOK'S NOTE
▲ This dip will need plenty of salt.
▲ Serve ready-prepared crudités with other dips available in supermarkets alongside this appetiser.

BLUE CHEESE AND PEAR HERO

A mouthwatering sandwich from dell'Ugo, one of London's trendiest eating places

1 small French loaf
olive oil or butter
2 ripe pears
about 150 g (5 oz) blue cheese or Gorgonzola
freshly grated Parmesan or pecorino cheese
dry breadcrumbs
SERVES 4

Slice loaf into 4 generous pieces. Brush each with olive oil or butter lightly. Core and slice pears thickly. Place on bread. Slice blue cheese thinly and place on top of pears. Sprinkle with Parmesan cheese and breadcrumbs. Grill until bubbling. Serve with lots of fresh watercress or a green salad.

COOK'S NOTES

▲ Thickly sliced rye bread or wholemeal bread may be used instead of French bread.

▲ If you find blue cheese too strongly flavoured, use feta cheese instead.

▲ Homemade breadcrumbs are far nicer than bought ones. Grate or process stale bread in a blender and freeze for later use.

SAUSAGE AND GREEN LENTIL CASSOULET

A wonderful French peasant dish that's guaranteed to keep the winter chill at bay

400 g (14 oz) green or brown lentils, cleaned
water to cover
1½ beef stock cubes
butter and sunflower oil for frying
1 large onion, chopped
2 cloves garlic, crushed (optional)
3 – 4 spicy smoked sausages, thickly sliced
15 ml (1 tbsp) wholegrain mustard
5 ml (1 tsp) mustard powder
45 ml (3 tbsp) white wine
5 ml (1 tsp) sugar
1 sprig fresh rosemary
salt and milled pepper
SERVES 4

Place lentils in water with crumbled stock cubes and bring to the boil. Reduce heat and simmer for 15 – 20 minutes. Meanwhile, heat butter and oil. Sauté onion and garlic until glossy. Add sausages and sauté for 1 minute. Add mustards and remaining ingredients and toss to coat. When lentils are just cooked, spoon lentil mixture, with juice, into pan. Simmer for 5 – 10 minutes, until heated through. Serve with vegetables.

SMOKED SALMON RISOTTO

This dish calls for a certain amount of attention, but preparation is minimal and the result is well worth the effort

- 45 ml (3 tbsp) butter
- 8 spring onions, chopped
- about 1.25 litres (2¼ pints) chicken stock, homemade (or use 1½ chicken stock cubes)
- 300 g (11 oz) arborio rice
- 45 ml (3 tbsp) vodka
- milled pepper
- 250 g (9 oz) smoked salmon offcuts
- 75 ml (5 tbsp) double cream
- 30 ml (2 tbsp) chopped fresh dill
- 60 ml (4 tbsp) freshly grated Parmesan cheese

SERVES 4

Melt butter, add spring onions and sauté until softened. Do not allow to brown. Heat stock to simmering point. Add rice to onion and stir. Add vodka, allow to bubble and almost evaporate. Add about a cupful of simmering stock, season with pepper. Cook rice over medium heat, adding stock as rice begins to dry out. When rice is *al dente* (25 – 30 minutes), stir in remaining ingredients. Season to taste and serve immediately.

COOK'S NOTES

▲ If you cannot find smoked salmon offcuts (at delicatessens or a seafood smokehouse), buy whole pieces and chop them.

▲ Arborio rice is available at any Italian delicatessen.

MEDITERRANEAN TART

Serve with a crisp green salad – or keep in the refrigerator for quick snacks

- 400 g (14 oz) frozen shortcrust pastry
- 45 ml (1 tbsp) wholegrain mustard
- 5 courgettes, sliced lengthways
- 4 tomatoes, seeded and thickly sliced
- 1 bunch spring onions, cut into 3 cm (1¼ inch) lengths
- 8 – 10 pitted black olives
- 3 large eggs
- 125 ml (4 fl oz) single cream
- 125 g (4 oz) ricotta cheese
- 60 ml (4 tbsp) Parmesan cheese
- 2 cloves garlic, crushed
- salt and milled pepper

SERVES 4

Roll pastry out to fit a greased 23 cm (9 inch) diameter flan tin. Cover pastry with waxed paper and fill with dried beans or rice. Bake blind at 200 °C (400 °F/gas 6) for 5 – 7 minutes. Remove beans or rice and paper and bake for a further 5 – 7 minutes. Cool slightly and spread mustard over base. Layer vegetables on top. Mix remaining ingredients together, pour over vegetables and sprinkle with a little extra Parmesan cheese. Bake at 200 °C (400 °F/gas 6) for 40 – 50 minutes, or until egg mixture has set. Serve hot, at room temperature, or cold.

TURKEY TACOS WITH AVO MAYO

When the thought of yet another turkey sandwich makes you blanch, go Mexican! Tacos are tasty, healthy and just plain fun

AVO MAYO
2 avocados, coarsely mashed
juice of ½ lemon
30 ml (2 tbsp) thick mayonnaise
15 ml (1 tbsp) thick natural yoghurt
salt, milled pepper and paprika to taste

TACOS
8 taco shells
about 16 slices turkey, chopped
½ iceberg lettuce, shredded
8 spring onions or 1 Spanish onion, chopped
4 tomatoes, chopped
SERVES 4

AVO MAYO: Mix all the ingredients together, adjusting lemon juice and seasoning according to taste. Reserve.
TACOS: Heat taco shells according to packet instructions. Fill shells with turkey and vegetables and top with a liberal dollop of avo mayo.

COOK'S NOTES

▲ Any chopped or shredded vegetables may be used in the filling. Some good options are cucumber, gherkins, peppers, pickled chillis and beansprouts.
▲ Cut calories by using more yoghurt and less mayonnaise in the avo mayo.
▲ Instead of turkey, leftover chicken can also be used in the taco filling.
▲ Taco shells are available from major supermarkets and delicatessens

ITALIAN PIZZA TOASTS

This is perfect as a quick and easy hors d'oeuvre to serve with drinks

8 slices French bread
sunflower or olive oil
2 large, ripe tomatoes
8 x 5 mm (¼ inch) thick slices
 mozzarella cheese
16 anchovies
olive oil
salt and milled pepper
SERVES 4

Brush bread with olive or sunflower oil and toast on 1 side. Slice tomatoes thickly. Place 1 – 2 slices tomato, 1 large slice cheese and 2 anchovies on untoasted side of bread slices. Drizzle with olive oil. Season toasts and grill until cheese melts. Serve while still hot.

COOK'S NOTES

▲ If you don't like anchovies, use thin slices of salami instead.

▲ Ciabatta or focaccia – both Italian breads – are perfect for this recipe but not as easily available as French bread.

▲ Serve with juicy black olives and fresh basil or watercress.

TORTILLA ESPAGNOL (SPANISH OMELETTE)

The traditional Spanish potato omelette may be eaten warm or at room temperature. Serve thick wedges with a salad as a light main course or cube and serve as hors d'oeuvres

175 – 250 ml (6 – 8 fl oz) olive and sunflower oil, mixed
750 g (1¾ lb) small potatoes, peeled and thinly sliced
2 medium onions, finely chopped
6 eggs, lightly beaten
salt and milled pepper
SERVES 4

Heat oil in a large heavy-based frying pan. Add potatoes and onions and fry, turning occasionally, until a light golden colour. (If you don't have a large enough pan to do this evenly in one go, cook in batches.) Drain potatoes and onions on paper towels. Pour off excess oil from pan, leaving a thin layer to coat base. When oil is hot, return potatoes and onions to pan, pour over eggs and season. Cook over moderate heat until base and sides are set. Continue cooking until done – about 2 – 3 minutes. (See Cook's Notes.).

COOK'S NOTES

▲ New potatoes may also be used. Traditionally, the potatoes are peeled but scrubbing will do just as well.

▲ Another way to prepare the tortilla is to bake it once you've sautéed the potatoes and onions. Place in an oven-to-table dish, pour over egg mixture and bake at 180 °C (350 °F/gas 4) for about 20 minutes.

▲ Chopped fresh rosemary added to the sautéed potatoes and onions gives a wonderful flavour.

ITALIAN-STYLE EGG NESTS

If you don't have an oven, the eggs can be poached separately and placed in the spinach 'nests'

1 kg (2¼ lb) spinach, washed
30 g (1 oz) butter
60 ml (4 tbsp) freshly grated Parmesan cheese
4 slices good quality Parma ham
4 small eggs
salt and milled pepper
SERVES 4

Cook spinach until leaves wilt. Chop and mix in butter and Parmesan cheese. Butter 4 ramekins or a large oven-to-table dish. Place spinach in dish and form 4 'nests'. (Dish should be small enough to ensure that spinach forms a deep layer.) Line each 'nest' with a slice of ham. Break 1 egg into each and season. Bake in a preheated 220 °C (425 °F/gas 7) oven until egg white is firm. Do not overcook. Serve immediately with fresh bread and a tomato salad.

COOK'S NOTES

▲ Pepper ham, thinly sliced baked ham, lightly grilled back bacon, smoked salmon or smoked salmon trout are all excellent alternatives to Parma ham.

FARMER'S OMELETTE

1 onion, diced
15 ml (1 tbsp) butter
6 rashers rindless bacon, diced
2 medium potatoes, cooked and diced
3 gherkins, chopped
6 mushrooms, cubed
2 large tomatoes, skinned, chopped and drained
6 jumbo eggs
125 ml (4 fl oz) water
salt and milled pepper
SERVES 4

Using a large, wide frying pan, sauté onion in butter until soft. Add bacon and sauté for about 3 minutes. Add all the vegetables and cook until just soft, about 6 minutes. Beat eggs, water and seasoning together and pour over vegetables. Stir once, briefly, to ensure an even spread of ingredients. Cook over low heat until just set, but not hard. It is important to remove omelette from hob just as it sets, as eggs will continue cooking and you could end up with a tough, rubbery omelette! Serve directly from pan with a fresh green salad.

COOK'S NOTES

▲ Ham, peppers and courgettes are also delicious in a farmer's omelette, so use whatever ingredients you have handy.

▲ Milk can be used instead of water. Milk gives a creamier flavour, but water will make a lighter omelette.

▲ The omelette can be browned lightly under the grill for a few seconds. Make sure the egg mixture is still very soft, otherwise the omelette will be overcooked.

FETA AND LEEK PANCAKES

8 pancakes
butter for frying

FILLING
10 – 12 rashers back bacon
butter and sunflower oil for frying
2 large leeks, cut into matchsticks
4 courgettes, cut into matchsticks
3.75 ml (¾ tsp) mustard powder
45 ml (3 tbsp) white wine
45 ml (3 tbsp) chicken or vegetable stock
3.75 ml (¾ tsp) sugar
salt and milled pepper
60 g (2 oz) crumbled feta cheese
SERVES 4

Gently fry pancakes in butter to heat through. Place in oven to keep warm. Grill or fry bacon rashers until crisp. Drain on paper towels to remove excess oil, crumble and set aside. Heat butter and oil in a large frying pan. Sauté leeks until just beginning to soften. Add courgettes. Toss to coat and add remaining ingredients, except feta. Cook until soft and liquid has evaporated. When required, remove pancakes from oven and preheat grill. Fill pancakes with vegetable mixture, crumbled bacon and feta cheese. Roll or fold pancakes, place in an ovenproof dish and sprinkle with feta cheese. Grill until cheese melts slightly and serve immediately.

CHEESE-'N-CORN TARTLETS

2 x 400 g (14 oz) packets shortcrust or flaky pastry

FILLING
425 g (15 oz) canned creamstyle sweetcorn
400 g (14 oz) canned whole kernel corn
125 g (4 oz) grated Cheddar cheese
2 large eggs
about 45 ml (3 tbsp) single cream
salt and milled pepper
SERVES 4

FILLING: Mix all ingredients together, reserving a little cheese. Grease 8 tartlet tins. Roll pastry out on a floured surface. Carefully ease pastry into tins and press well into sides. Trim and neaten edges. If using shortcrust pastry, brush pastry with a little egg yolk and bake blind at 200 °C (400 °F/gas 6) for 10 minutes (See Cook's Notes). Spoon filling mixture into pastry cases and sprinkle cheese over. Bake at 180 °C (350 °F/gas 4) for 20 – 30 minutes, or until set and golden. If using flaky pastry, bake on second shelf from the bottom of the oven at 220 °C (425 °F/gas 7) for 20 – 30 minutes.

COOK'S NOTES

▲ To bake blind, cover pastry with discs of waxed paper; top with dried beans or rice (to hold the pastry down) and bake as directed. Remove beans or rice and paper and allow to cool. Baking blind is not recommended for puff pastry.

▲ One large tart may be made, but you will only need 1 packet of pastry. The baking time remains the same.

BASIL AND TOMATO BRUSCHETTA

1 French loaf
olive or sunflower oil
1 clove garlic, peeled
6 large, very ripe, tomatoes
3 cloves garlic, crushed
15 – 20 ml (3 – 4 tsp) olive oil
2.5 – 5 ml (½ – 1 tsp) sugar
salt and milled pepper
1 large bunch fresh basil, sage or oregano
SERVES 10 – 15 AS AN APPETIZER

Slice bread, brush with oil and rub with garlic clove (or, better still, brush with garlic-flavoured oil). Bake in a pre-heated oven at 180 °C (350 °F/gas 4) for 20 – 25 minutes or until golden and crisp. Cool on wire racks. Immerse tomatoes in boiling water for about 2 minutes to loosen skins. Skin tomatoes and chop flesh very finely. Add garlic, olive oil and seasoning. Spoon a liberal amount on to each slice, garnish with basil, sage or oregano leaf and serve with drinks.

COOK'S NOTES

▲ Ricotta or mozzarella cheese may be sliced and placed under the tomato mixture.

▲ Watch the bruschetta closely while they are baking to ensure they do not burn.

NEW YEAR TURKEY

Leftover Christmas turkey can definitely get very boring, so here's a new and delicious way to liven it up!

1 large French loaf
good quality mayonnaise
8 slices leftover roast turkey
8 rashers back bacon, grilled until crisp
sweet chutney and watercress
SERVES 4

Divide the bread into 4 pieces. Slice open and spread with a liberal amount of mayonnaise. Top with turkey and bacon. Garnish with watercress and drizzle with hot, sweet chutney.

COOK'S NOTES

▲ Any sort of bread may be used, but crusty white bread is best.

▲ Leftover roast chicken is also perfect for this sandwich. If there isn't enough leftover meat to slice, shred it instead.

▲ If you don't have leftovers, simply poach chicken or turkey breasts in chicken stock, remove skin and slice.

▲ Grilled bresaola may replace the bacon.

HAKE CAKES WITH AVOCADO SALSA

500 g (18 oz) hake, steamed and flaked
1 onion, finely chopped
30 ml (2 tbsp) chopped chives
75 ml (5 tbsp) chopped parsley
15 – 20 ml (3 – 4 tsp) lemon juice
salt and milled pepper
1 egg, lightly beaten
breadcrumbs or sesame seeds to coat

SALSA
2.5 ml (½ tsp) chilli flakes
juice of ½ small lemon
1 – 2 ripe avocados, mashed
salt and milled pepper
45 ml (3 tbsp) chopped coriander (optional)
10 ml (2 tsp) olive or sunflower oil
SERVES 4

Soak chilli flakes in lemon juice for a few minutes to soften. Mix all salsa ingredients together; set aside. Mix all fish cake ingredients together, except breadcrumbs. Using your hands mould about 8 patties. Cover with cling film and chill. Heat butter and oil in a pan. Coat fish cakes on both sides with crumbs and pat gently to remove excess. Fry on both sides until golden. Remove from pan; place on paper towels in warming drawer. Cook all cakes and serve with avocado salsa.

MUSSELS IN CREAM AND WINE

about 45 ml (3 tbsp) butter
1 large onion, chopped
1 bunch parsley, chopped
4 cloves garlic, crushed
15 ml (1 tbsp) plain flour
125 ml (4 fl oz) white wine
250 ml (8 fl oz) chicken stock, made with 1 cube
5 ml (1 tsp) sugar
salt and milled pepper
about 48 mussels in shells (12 mussels per person)
200 ml (7 fl oz) single cream
SERVES 4

Melt butter in a large saucepan. Sauté onion, parsley and garlic until glossy. Stir in flour and cook through. Slowly pour in wine and stock. Add sugar and season to taste. Bring to the boil. Reduce heat and simmer for 10 minutes. Add mussels, cover and steam until shells open. Remove mussels with a slotted spoon and place them in a heated serving dish. (Any mussels that do not open must be thrown away.) Add cream to remaining stock and bring to the boil. Remove from heat immediately and pour over mussels. Serve with crusty bread and a green salad.

COOK'S NOTES

▲ If you gather your own mussels, soak them in cold water for about 10 minutes after cleaning to remove grit.
▲ Store-bought mussels with their shells already open are pre-cooked, and need only be heated through.

FISH WITH CREAM OF TOMATO AND BASIL SAUCE

4 fresh fish cutlets, such as cod
juice of 1 lemon
salt and milled pepper
about 20 g (¾ oz) butter

SAUCE
olive oil for frying
2 bunches spring onions, chopped
3 large, ripe tomatoes, peeled, seeded and chopped
2.5 ml (½ tsp) sugar
about 200 ml (7 fl oz) soured cream
45 g (1½ oz) torn fresh basil leaves
salt, milled pepper and lemon juice to taste
SERVES 4

Wipe fish with a damp cloth. Sprinkle with lemon juice and season. Dot each cutlet with a little butter and grill for 3 – 5 minutes on each side, depending on thickness. Heat oil in a pan and sauté spring onions for 1 – 2 minutes; add tomatoes and sugar. Cook for a further 2 minutes and add soured cream. Bring just to the boil and remove immediately from hob. Stir in basil and season to taste. Spoon a little sauce over each cutlet and serve with baby potatoes and steamed vegetables.

COOK'S NOTES

▲ If you can't find fresh basil, use the same quantity of fresh dill.

SQUID WITH BLACK BUTTER

Squid with the slightly burnt flavour of garlic and lemon butter, enjoyed with a glass of crisp white wine, is a taste experience not to be missed. Serve as a starter with crusty bread or with lemony rice and salad as a main course

300 – 400 g (11 – 14 oz) squid tubes
45 g (1½ oz) butter
15 ml (1 tbsp) olive oil
4 cloves garlic, sliced
7.5 ml (1½ tsp) crushed chilli (optional)
juice of 1 small lemon
salt and milled pepper
SERVES 4

Wash squid thoroughly, making sure that you remove the thin, plastic-looking spine in the centre. Pat dry. Heat butter and oil in a large pan or wok. Add garlic and chilli and sauté over high heat for about 1 minute. Add squid and stir-fry for about 1 minute. Add lemon juice and seasoning and fry for a further minute. Serve immediately with crusty bread for mopping up the juices.

COOK'S NOTES

▲ If using chilli, garnish with fresh coriander.

▲ You will need 750 – 900 g (1¾ – 2 lb) squid tubes for a main course serving. Double all the other ingredients.

GRILLED FISH WITH SALSA VERDE

575 – 750 g (1¼ – 1¾ lb) fish of your choice, filleted
15 ml (1 tbsp) lemon juice
15 ml (1 tbsp) butter
salt and milled pepper

SALSA VERDE
2 large gherkins, chopped
30 ml (2 tbsp) chopped capers
12 – 15 green olives, stoned and chopped
30 ml (2 tbsp) pesto (see (see Cook's Notes)
60 ml (4 tbsp) chopped parsley
2 cloves garlic, crushed (optional)
5 – 7.5 ml (1 –1½ tsp) lemon juice
3.75 ml (¾ tsp) sugar
30 ml (2 tbsp) olive oil
salt and milled pepper
SERVES 4

Wipe fish with a damp cloth. Line a baking sheet with foil, shiny side up, and crumple the edges so that no cooking juices escape. Place fish on foil. Sprinkle with lemon juice, dot with butter and season. Preheat grill and grill fish on lower rack for 15 – 20 minutes, or until fish flakes easily. Meanwhile, mix all salsa ingredients together. Fresh dill or basil (as much as you like) may also be added. Serve salsa separately or place about 15 ml (1 tbsp) on top of each portion.

COOK'S NOTES

▲ The salsa is wonderful with any fish, whether it is barbecued, grilled, baked, filleted or whole.

▲ The salsa may be made at least a day in advance, then covered with clingwrap and refrigerated.

▲ Pesto can be bought at most large delicatessens and keeps for quite a few months in the refrigerator. Alternatively you can make it yourself: Purée 20 g (¾ oz) basil leaves, 3 cloves garlic, 15 ml (1 tbsp) pine kernels, 60 g (2 oz) Parmesan cheese, 100 – 250 ml (3½ – 8 fl oz) olive oil until smooth, adding only enough oil to incorporate well.

GRILLED FISH WITH TOMATO-BASIL BUTTER

about 750 g (1¾ lb) white fish fillets
45 ml (3 tbsp) olive oil
juice of ½ lemon
salt and milled pepper

TOMATO-BASIL BUTTER
45 g (1½ oz) softened butter
15 ml (1 tbsp) chopped fresh basil
10 ml (2 tsp) lemon juice
about 10 ml (2 tsp) tomato paste
2.5 ml (½ tsp) wholegrain mustard
pinch sugar (optional)
SERVES 4

Wipe fish with a clean, damp cloth and place in a shallow baking dish. Mix olive oil and lemon juice, season to taste and pour over fish. Marinate while preparing flavoured butter.

TOMATO-BASIL BUTTER: Mix all ingredients together. Add extra tomato paste, if desired, for a good red colour. Shape as desired (see Cook's Notes). Wrap in waxed paper or cling film and freeze while cooking fish. (If you make butter a few hours ahead of time, you will only need to refrigerate it.) Grill fish for 5 – 8 minutes, depending on the thickness. To check if it is done, flake with a fork or skewer – the flesh should flake easily. Place fish on plates and top with a pat of butter. Serve with a fresh salad or steamed young vegetables.

COOK'S NOTES

▲ Sage or rosemary may be used instead of basil, but then serve with a fuller-flavoured fish like tuna or mackerel.

▲ Use a melon baller to make easy butter shapes. Or roll butter into a sausage, wrap in cling film or waxed paper and chill until firm before cutting into rounds. You can also press the butter into a square, wrap and chill and then slice or shave off pieces.

▲ Margarine cannot be used instead of the butter as it doesn't have the right flavour and will not harden sufficiently when chilled.

▲ Leftover flavoured butter will keep for up to 3 months in the freezer.

SWEET AND SOUR APRICOT FISH

575 – 750 g (1¼ – 1¾ lb) firm–fleshed fish, filleted
butter and sunflower oil for frying
about 500 – 600 ml (17 fl oz – 1 pint) pure apricot juice
2 cloves garlic, crushed (optional)
5 ml (1 tsp) each ground coriander and cumin
salt and milled pepper
SERVES 4

Wipe fish with a damp cloth. Heat butter and oil and fry fish on both sides until golden. Remove from pan and keep warm. Pour apricot juice into pan, increase heat and bring the juice to the boil. Add garlic, spices and seasoning. Cook, stirring constantly to incorporate pan scrapings, until juice is reduced to a slightly thickened sauce (about 5 – 6 minutes' furious boiling). Reduce heat, add fish and simmer for 8 – 10 minutes, or until heated through.

COOK'S NOTES

▲ Any firm-fleshed fish may be used for this recipe; dogfish is very good.
▲ To add a lightly curried flavour to this dish, add about 15 ml (1 tbsp) of strong curry powder to the butter and oil before frying the fish.
▲ Dried apricots may be added to the sauce for an extra dash of interest. If the dried apricots are slightly hard, they will need to be soaked in a little hot water before cooking.

CHINESE FISH KEBABS

about 1 kg (2¼ lb) firm white fish, filleted
juice of 1 orange
juice of ½ lemon
60 ml (4 tbsp) soy sauce
2.5 ml (½ tsp) finely chopped fresh ginger, or 5 ml (1 tsp) dried
60 ml (4 tbsp) sesame seeds
15 ml (1 tbsp) honey or sugar
SERVES 4 (2 KEBABS EACH)

Wipe fish with a damp cloth and cut into 2 cm (¾ inch) cubes. Thread about 6 cubes each on to 8 thin skewers. Mix remaining ingredients together. If time allows, marinate kebabs in mixture for at least 30 minutes. Place on a baking sheet and grill for 2 minutes. Turn kebabs, baste and grill for a further 2 minutes. Heat remaining sauce and spoon over kebabs. Serve with a salad or lightly steamed vegetables.

COOK'S NOTES

▲ Marinating is not essential but it does enhance the flavour. If you're in a hurry, just baste the kebabs liberally before and during grilling.

▲ Ready in under 15 minutes, including preparation, fish kebabs are an excellent source of protein.

▲ Cubed squid steaks can be used as an alternative, but will cost much more.

HAKE EN PAPILLOTE

750 g (1¾ lb) hake, filleted and cut into 4 portions
4 slim leeks, washed well
4 courgettes
2 medium carrots, peeled
60 ml (4 tbsp) olive oil
juice of 1 lemon
pinch sugar
3.75 ml (¾ tsp) mustard powder
½ chicken or vegetable stock cube, crumbled
15 ml (1 tbsp) green peppercorns (optional)
salt and milled pepper
SERVES 4

Wash hake and pat dry. Cut leeks in half, slice lengthways so that 'leaves' are separate. Slice courgettes and carrots into thin matchsticks. Cut foil into 4 pieces (about 20 x 20 cm/8 x 8 inches). Place shiny side up. Place a hake portion in centre of each and top with vegetables. Whisk remaining ingredients together (if you don't use green peppercorns, add about 15 ml (1 tbsp) fresh dill or oregano). Pour oil mixture over fish and seal parcels. Bake in a 180 °C (350 °F/gas 4) preheated oven for 20 – 30 minutes, depending on thickness. (Flesh should be opaque and flake quite easily.) Remove and serve, in parcels, accompanied by rice, potatoes or lentils cooked in a little stock.

COOK'S NOTES

▲ Other firm-fleshed fish can be used instead of hake. Boned chicken breasts are also delicious cooked this way.

COCONUT-CRUSTED FISH WITH MANGO SALSA

45 g (1½ oz) desiccated coconut
15 g (½ oz) butter
45 ml (3 tbsp) single cream
2.5 ml (½ tsp) fresh ginger
salt
4 x 200 g (7 oz) hake fillets, cleaned

SALSA
1 large mango
1 fresh green or red chilli
1 small onion, finely chopped
juice of ½ lemon
1.25 ml (¼ tsp) sugar
salt and milled pepper
¼ bunch fresh coriander, chopped (optional)
SERVES 4

Mix coconut, butter, cream, ginger and salt together. Spread a layer of coconut mixture over each fish fillet. Line a baking sheet with foil, shiny side up, and crumple edges to prevent juices escaping. Place fish on foil. Preheat grill and grill fish until cooked, 20 – 25 minutes, depending on thickness of fillets. Flesh should be opaque and firm to the touch.
SALSA: Mix ingredients and macerate while fish is cooking. Serve as an accompaniment to the fish.

SKATE WITH CITRUS BUTTER

A seldom thought of, but delicious and inexpensive fish, combined here with a citrus butter for extra zing

4 x 200 g (7 oz) skate wings
45 g (1½ oz) butter
15 ml (1 tbsp) sunflower oil
juice of 1 lemon
juice of 2 oranges
salt and milled pepper
30 ml (2 tbsp) chopped parsley
thinly sliced peel of 1 lemon and 1 orange
SERVES 4

Wipe skate wings with a damp cloth. Heat butter and oil in a large frying pan and sauté skate for about 4 minutes on each side. Add juices, seasoning and parsley. Reduce heat, cover and cook for a further 5 minutes or until done. Place fish on heated plates, pour over butter and top with sliced citrus peel. Serve with crisp, stir-fried vegetables.

COOK'S NOTES

▲ Any other white fish may be used instead of the skate.

▲ For extra crunch, sprinkle breadcrumbs over cooked fish and grill for a minute or two.

SMOKED HADDOCK WITH PARSLEY POTATOES

30 g (1 oz) butter
1 large onion, sliced
4 peppercorns
2 bay leaves
5 ml (1 tsp) mustard powder
200 ml (7 fl oz) milk
60 ml (4 tbsp) single cream
500 g (18 oz) smoked haddock
6 potatoes, diced
45 – 60 ml (3 – 4 tbsp) chopped parsley
salt and pepper
SERVES 4

Heat butter and sauté onion until glossy. Add next 5 ingredients. Bring to just below boiling point. Add haddock and poach gently until cooked through (liquid should not cover fish). Remove haddock and onion with a slotted spoon, pour a little poaching liquid over and keep warm. Meanwhile, boil potatoes in another saucepan until soft, about 20 minutes. Drain. Remove peppercorns and bay leaves from poaching liquid and mash potatoes with liquid. Add extra butter, milk and seasoning if needed. Stir parsley into potatoes and mix well. Spoon or pipe mashed potatoes on to plate next to fish and serve with steamed vegetables.

COOK'S NOTES

▲ The poached haddock may be placed in a flameproof dish, topped with mashed potatoes and grilled until lightly browned.

PAN-FRIED TROUT WITH SAGE

This recipe works best with trout, but any small whole fish may be used. Don't stint on the butter: it gives the dish its sweet, slightly burnt flavour

4 trout, each 200 – 250 g (7 – 8 oz)
flour for dusting
90 g (3 oz) butter
4 bay leaves
about 10 sage leaves
60 ml (4 tbsp) dry white wine
60 ml (4 tbsp) brandy
SERVES 4

Wash trout and pat dry. Dust lightly with flour, patting fish gently to remove any excess. Heat butter, bay leaves and sage in a large pan. (You may want to divide the ingredients in 2 and use 2 pans to cook the trout, so that all 4 may be served together.) When butter is golden brown, add trout and fry over high heat, turning once, until skin is crisp and golden. Reduce heat slightly and add wine and brandy. Cook for a further 5 minutes. Serve immediately, garnished with crisp sage and bay leaves. Boiled baby potatoes and a tomato salad are the perfect accompaniments.

COOK'S NOTES

▲ Don't substitute dried sage for fresh. Fresh herbs are available at delicatessens and greengrocers.

▲ If possible, buy fresh, not frozen fish for pan frying.

WHITE FISH WITH CORIANDER CREAM

butter for frying
1 small green chilli, finely chopped
2 x 200 g (7 oz) white fish fillets
juice of 1 small lemon
about 20 g (¾ oz) minced coriander
about 125 ml (4 fl oz) single cream
salt and milled pepper
SERVES 4

Melt butter and lightly sauté chilli for a minute or two. Add fish and brown on one side. Turn down heat, cover pan with a lid and cook for about 3 minutes. Add lemon juice and cook for a further 2 minutes. The fish should be just cooked. Stir in coriander and cream, season and cook over high heat for about 1 minute. Serve immediately with tagliarini tossed with fresh lemon juice, olive oil and milled pepper. Garnish with fresh coriander.

COOK'S NOTES

▲ Any firm-fleshed white fish such as cod can be used.

▲ Place the fresh coriander in a food processor and blend to form a purée.

CHICKEN PROVENCALE

4 boned, skinned chicken breasts
salt and milled pepper
10 ml (2 tsp) mustard powder
15 ml (1 tbsp) olive oil
1 large onion, finely chopped
4 cloves garlic, crushed
400 g (14 oz) canned whole peeled tomatoes, chopped, juice retained
7.5 ml (1½ tsp) sugar
30 ml (2 tbsp) white wine
10 ml (2 tsp) dried tarragon or basil
butter and oil for frying
5 ml (1 tsp) mustard seeds
SERVES 4

Clean chicken breasts and pat dry with paper towels. Season with salt, pepper and 5 ml (1 tsp) mustard powder, set aside. Heat olive oil and sauté onion and garlic until glossy. Add tomatoes, sugar, remaining mustard powder, wine and tarragon. Bring to the boil, then reduce heat and simmer. Heat butter and oil in another frying pan. Add mustard seeds and, when they are just beginning to pop, add the chicken and cook for 3 – 4 minutes on both sides. Season tomato sauce to taste and serve over chicken breasts.

SPICY SESAME CHICKEN WINGS

16 chicken wings
45 ml (3 tbsp) honey
15 ml (1 tbsp) sieved apricot jam
90 ml (6 tbsp) soy sauce
juice of ½ orange
juice of ½ lemon
2.5 – 5 ml (½ – 1 tsp) ground ginger
3 cloves garlic, crushed
5 ml (1 tsp) mustard powder
milled pepper
45 ml (3 tbsp) sesame seeds
SERVES 4

Wash chicken wings and pat dry. Set aside. Mix all other ingredients together in a large bowl. Toss wings in sauce to coat and, if possible, allow to marinate for 1 – 2 hours. If time is short, this step is not absolutely necessary. Remove from marinade and thread on to skewers, 3 – 4 wings to each. Place in a roasting tin and pour over excess marinade. Bake at 180 °C (350 °F/gas 4) for 25 – 30 minutes or grill, turning and basting every 5 minutes for a total of 20 minutes. Remove from oven and serve with new potatoes and salad.

GARLIC YOGHURT CHICKEN

1.5 kg (3 lb) chicken portions

MARINADE
about 200 ml (7 fl oz) natural yoghurt
5 cloves garlic, crushed
juice of 1 small lemon
30 ml (2 tbsp) honey
5 ml (1 tsp) each salt and milled pepper
1 bunch chives, finely chopped
SERVES 4

MARINADE: Mix all ingredients together and reserve.
Wash chicken, pat dry and set aside. Preheat grill. Place chicken on rack of grill pan. Grill for 6 minutes on each side. Liberally brush yoghurt marinade over each portion of chicken and grill for 5 minutes, turn over and repeat the basting and turning process 3 times, (the skin of the chicken will look very charred, but it will taste marvellous!).

COOK'S NOTES

▲ Buying a whole chicken and cutting it into portions is cheaper than buying already cut portions.

APRICOT CHICKEN KEBABS

200 ml (7 fl oz) unsweetened apricot juice
32 dried apricots
8 chicken kebabs
2 – 3 large onions
salt and milled pepper
10 ml (2 tsp) mustard powder
2.5 ml (½ tsp) each ground cumin and coriander
30 ml (2 tbsp) semi-sweet white wine
SERVES 4 – 6

Heat apricot juice, remove from hob and soak apricots in it until softened. Remove chicken pieces from skewers. Chop onions into eighths. Thread cubed chicken on to skewers, alternately with apricots and onion. Place on a baking sheet. Stir remaining ingredients into leftover apricot juice and pour over kebabs. Preheat grill, place kebabs on grill rack and cook for about 5 minutes. Turn kebabs over, baste with juice and cook for a further 5 minutes. Serve with baked potatoes and a salad.

COOK'S NOTES

▲ Cubed chicken on skewers is available at many large supermarkets. Buying kebabs, and making your own sauce, is cheaper than buying the ready-prepared convenience food.

▲ A packet of 4 kebabs will, when apricots and onions are added, make about 6 portions.

MUSTARD CREAM CHICKEN BREASTS

4 boned, skinned chicken breasts
plain flour
20 ml (4 tsp) sunflower oil
10 ml (2 tsp) butter
10 ml (2 tsp) light mustard seeds
15 – 20 ml (3 – 4 tsp) mustard powder
60 ml (4 tbsp) wholegrain mustard
60 ml (4 tbsp) white wine
200 ml (7 fl oz) single cream
5 ml (1 tsp) sugar
salt to taste
SERVES 4

Wipe chicken breasts with a damp cloth, dust lightly with flour and set aside. Heat oil and butter and add mustard seeds. When seeds begin to pop, place chicken in pan and brown on both sides. Mix remaining ingredients together and add to pan. Bring to boiling point (do not boil), then simmer for about 7 minutes. Serve with noodles or rice and a salad.

COOK'S NOTES

▲ Natural yoghurt or half cream, half yoghurt may be used for the mustard cream. The appearance will then be slightly grainy but the chicken will taste just as good.

▲ Any good French mustard can be used.

▲ Mustard seeds are available at large supermarkets and speciality spice shops.

FRICASSEED CHICKEN WITH BACON AND APPLES

Adding a few rashers of bacon gives this trouble-free dish a robust, smoky flavour

- 3 – 4 rashers rindless streaky bacon, chopped
- 2 large onions, quartered and broken into shells
- olive oil
- 8 chicken thighs, skinned
- flour for dusting
- 5 ml (1 tsp) mustard powder
- salt and milled pepper
- 600 – 750 ml (1 – 1¾ pints) chicken stock (use 2 cubes)
- 60 ml (4 tbsp) white wine
- 5 ml (1 tsp) sugar
- 2 bay leaves
- 2 Granny Smith apples, peeled, cored and cut into eighths

SERVES 4

Sauté bacon lightly in a frying pan or saucepan for about 3 minutes. Add onions and a little olive oil. Sauté until glossy. Dust chicken lightly with flour and add to pan. Sauté on both sides until lightly golden. Add remaining ingredients, except apples. Cover and bring to the boil. Reduce heat, add apples and simmer for 20 minutes. Turn chicken, cover and cook for a further 15 – 20 minutes, or until done. Serve with rice and vegetables.

COOK'S NOTES

▲ Chicken breasts, skinned but not boned, may be used instead of thighs but halve them to ensure even cooking.

▲ For an all-in-one meal – and if your pan is large enough – add 12 – 16 baby potatoes, halved, when you add the stock.

CHICKEN BREASTS WITH HERBS

4 – 6 boned, skinned chicken breasts
strong chicken stock to cover
celery leaves
1 onion
black peppercorns
1 bay leaf

SAUCE
150 ml (¼ pint) thick yoghurt
150 ml (¼ pint) soured cream
15 ml (1 tbsp) mayonnaise
15 ml (1 tbsp) lemon juice
2.5 cloves garlic, crushed
bunch chives, dill or basil
½ bunch parsley, chopped
2.5 ml (½ tsp) mustard powder
salt and milled pepper
SERVES 4

Arrange breasts in a large pan, pour over chicken stock, add celery leaves, onion, peppercorns and bay leaf, cover and bring to a gentle simmer. Simmer for about 10 – 12 minutes, until just cooked through. Remove from heat and, if time allows, cool in broth. Remove and chill. Meanwhile, mix sauce ingredients together. Slice breasts, pour over sauce and garnish with lemon wedges, watercress and salad leaves.

SWEET AND SOUR LIME CHICKEN

A delicious chicken recipe that may be baked or grilled. The flavour of ginger and coriander adds an oriental touch

grated rind of 1 lime
125 ml (4 fl oz) lime juice
250 ml (8 fl oz) freshly squeezed orange juice
60 ml (4 tbsp) honey
7.5 ml (1½ tsp) dried or 5 ml (1 tsp) fresh chopped ginger
½ bunch coriander, chopped
salt and milled pepper
8 chicken portions
SERVES 4

Mix all ingredients except chicken together. If baking, marinate chicken in mixture for at least 1 hour. Bake at 180 °C (350 °F/gas 4) for about 40 minutes. If grilling, grill for 6 minutes a side without basting. Then baste with the honey mixture and turn every 5 minutes for a total of 15 – 20 minutes. (Don't worry if the chicken skin seems to burn; the honey causes caramelization and the skin is sweet and delicious.) Serve with a crisp mixed salad and a baked potato, or steamed vegetables and rice.

COOK'S NOTES

▲ Grated lemon rind and fresh lemon juice may be used if limes are not available.

▲ This chicken marinade can also be used as a delicious basting sauce on a barbecue.

TURKEY CROQUETTES

These crisp croquettes are the answer for using up leftover Christmas turkey (or chicken)

1 onion, finely diced
sunflower oil and butter for frying
300 g (11 oz) cooked turkey or chicken
150 g (5 oz) mixed cooked leftover vegetables
2 potatoes, cooked
1 egg
salt and milled pepper
cornflake crumbs or breadcrumbs to coat
sunflower oil for frying
SERVES 4

Sauté onion in a little oil and butter until glossy. Shred meat and chop or mash vegetables and potatoes. Mix with onion and egg. Season to taste. Roll into croquettes, coat with cornflake crumbs and chill for about 10 minutes. (Chilling helps to prevent crumbs falling off during frying.) Heat oil and fry croquettes on both sides until golden, about 8 minutes. Serve with cranberry sauce and vegetables.

COOK'S NOTES

▲ Any selection of vegetables may be used in the filling.
▲ Leftover stuffing may also be added to the mixture. If it is too heavy, fold in 1 beaten egg white.
▲ If you have no leftover vegetables, boil 2 large carrots, 1 stalk of celery and 3 courgettes and chop or mash before use.

MARMALADE MUSTARD CHICKEN

8 chicken pieces
a few sprigs fresh rosemary

BASTING SAUCE
60 ml (4 tbsp) Seville orange marmalade
30 ml (2 tbsp) wholegrain mustard
30 ml (2 tbsp) prepared English mustard
60 ml (4 tbsp) orange juice
60 ml (4 tbsp) chicken stock (use 1 cube)
15 ml (1 tbsp) mustard seeds
salt and milled pepper
SERVES 4

Mix all basting sauce ingredients. Set aside. Wipe chicken with a damp cloth and place in an oven-to-table dish. Pour mixture over chicken pieces, add rosemary and cover with foil, shiny side in. Bake at 180 °C (350 °F/gas 4) for 30 minutes. Remove foil, baste chicken and continue to bake for a further 20 – 30 minutes. Serve with new potatoes and a salad.

COOK'S NOTES

▲ To cut down on fat, skin the chicken pieces before baking.
▲ This dish may also be cooked on the hob in a large frying pan, covered. This method will shorten the cooking time by about 20 minutes.
▲ To make a wonderful basting sauce for barbecued or grilled chicken or chops, follow the recipe for the sauce, omitting the stock and half the orange juice.

LIGHTLY CURRIED YOGHURT CHICKEN

1.5 kg (3 lb) skinned chicken, cut into 8 portions
5 ml (1 tsp) turmeric
10 ml (2 tsp) ground cumin
10 ml (2 tsp) mustard powder
15 ml (1 tbsp) medium curry powder
60 ml (4 tbsp) mango chutney
5 ml (1 tsp) ground ginger (optional)
salt
100 ml (3½ fl oz) white wine
75 ml (5 tbsp) apricot or orange juice
500 ml (17 fl oz) natural yoghurt
10 – 15 ml (2 – 3 tsp) cornflour
  mixed to a paste with milk
SERVES 4 – 6

Arrange chicken in an oven-to-table dish. Mix all ingredients, except cornflour and milk, thoroughly and pour over chicken. Marinate for at least 1 hour. Cover with foil and bake for 35 minutes in a preheated 160 °C (325 °F/gas 3) oven. Uncover and bake for a further 30 minutes. Remove from oven and stir in cornflour and milk mixture. Return to oven and bake for a further 10 minutes, or until cornflour is cooked through, sauce is thickened and chicken is tender. Alternatively, bake chicken as instructed, adding 10 minutes to cooking time. Remove from oven. Pour curry sauce into a saucepan, thicken with cornflour over low heat and pour over chicken. Serve with rice.

FESTIVE CHICKEN

Join the Christmas spirit with this boozy, fruity chicken dish

sunflower oil for frying
1 large onion, chopped
8 chicken pieces
250 ml (8 fl oz) chicken stock made with 1 cube
45 – 60 ml (3 – 4 tbsp) orange juice
about 60 g (2 oz) seedless raisins
about 60 g (2 oz) pecan nuts
salt and milled pepper
60 – 90 ml (4 – 6 tbsp) sherry
SERVES 4

Heat oil and sauté onion for a few minutes. Add chicken and brown on all sides. Add stock and orange juice and bring to the boil. Reduce heat, add raisins, nuts and seasoning and simmer for about 20 minutes. Increase heat, stir in sherry to taste and cook for a further 3 – 4 minutes. Serve with steamed vegetables and roast potatoes or rice.

COOK'S NOTES

▲ Don't use too much oil when frying the onions as the chicken skin also gives off fat and the dish will end up very oily.
▲ Almonds or hazelnuts may be used instead of pecans.

CHICKEN BREASTS WITH CURRIED FRUIT MAYONNAISE

butter and oil for frying
4 chicken breast fillets
15 ml (1 tbsp) each ground cumin and coriander
salt to taste

MAYONNAISE
about 15 ml (1 tbsp) sunflower oil
1 small onion, chopped
15 ml (1 tbsp) medium-strength curry powder
5 ml (1 tsp) each ground cumin and coriander
60 ml (4 tbsp) mango chutney
60 g (2 oz) raisins soaked in 60 ml (4 tbsp)
apricot or orange juice
125 ml (4 fl oz) good quality mayonnaise
125 ml (4 fl oz) thick natural yoghurt
SERVES 4

MAYONNAISE: Heat oil in a frying pan. Sauté onion for 1 minute. Add curry powder, cumin and coriander and sauté for about 3 minutes. As mixture begins to clump together, slowly stir in chutney, raisins and juice. Cook for 1 – 2 minutes. Cool slightly. Stir into mayonnaise and yoghurt and set aside.
Heat butter and oil in pan. Coat chicken in spices and season with salt. Fry until cooked through, about 3 minutes on both sides. Serve hot with fruit mayonnaise.

SOUTHERN FRIED CHICKEN

A traditional American dish from Down South

8 chicken pieces
2 eggs
30 ml (2 tbsp) water
125 g (4 oz) plain flour
125 g (4 oz) cornmeal
5 ml (1 tsp) paprika
salt and milled pepper
sunflower oil for frying
SERVES 4

Wash chicken and pat dry. Beat egg and water together. Mix flour, cornmeal, paprika and seasoning together. Heat oil in a deep frying pan or fryer (to 180 °C/350°F), until hot but not smoking. Dip chicken pieces into egg mixture, then coat them with flour mixture. Shake off excess. Deep fry in small batches until golden and crisp. Take care not to undercook the chicken; it should take 12 – 20 minutes. Drain on a wire rack. Serve hot or at room temperature with chips and braised okra.

COOK'S NOTES

▲ If you use light meat instead of dark, the chicken will cook in about a third of the time.
▲ The cooked chicken may be kept warm in the oven.

CHICKEN PAPRIKA

4 boned, skinned and trimmed chicken breasts
lemon juice
salt and milled pepper
60 g (2 oz) butter
2 medium onions, very finely chopped
20 ml (4 tsp) paprika
60 ml (4 tbsp) red wine
60 ml (4 tbsp) chicken stock
125 – 150 ml (4 – 5 fl oz) natural yoghurt
parsley to garnish
SERVES 4

Preheat oven to 200 °C (400 °F/gas 6). Pat chicken breasts dry on paper towels. Sprinkle with lemon juice and pepper. Heat 45 g (1½ oz) butter in a heavy-based frying pan. Brown chicken on both sides and remove with a slotted spoon. Add remaining butter and brown chopped onions well. Add salt to taste. Add paprika, wine and stock, stir well and cook gently until slightly reduced. Place chicken breasts in an ovenproof dish and pour over paprika sauce, distributing evenly. Bake for 15 – 20 minutes, taking care not to overcook chicken. Stir in yoghurt just before serving and sprinkle with chopped parsley.

COOK'S NOTES

▲ Don't overcook the chicken breasts – they will become dry.

▲ The chicken may also be prepared in a casserole dish which can go straight from the hob into the oven.

▲ Serve the chicken with potatoes and a crisp salad.

CREAM CHEESE AND SAGE CHICKEN BREASTS

The sage, garlic and lemon flavours seep into the chicken breasts, leaving you with an aromatic and superbly moist dish.

4 chicken breasts
lemon juice
salt and milled pepper

FILLING
200 g (7 oz) curd cheese
juice and grated rind of ½ lemon
30 ml (2 tbsp) chopped fresh sage or 15 ml (1 tbsp) dried
4 – 5 cloves garlic, crushed
5 ml (1 tsp) mustard powder
salt and milled pepper
SERVES 4

Preheat oven to 200 °C (400 °F/gas 6). Mix all filling ingredients together well. With your fingers, lift skin away from meat on 1 side of each chicken breast. Gently ease cream cheese filling under skin. If necessary, secure open side with a cocktail stick. (This may be done a day in advance, covered with waxed paper and refrigerated until 1 hour before roasting.) Squeeze lemon juice over chicken, season and place in a roasting pan. Cover with foil, shiny side in, and roast for 15 minutes. Remove foil and roast for a further 10 minutes. When a skewer is inserted, juices should run clear. Serve with roast potatoes and/or steamed vegetables.

COOK'S NOTES

▲ If you are diet conscious, use low-fat cheese in the filling.

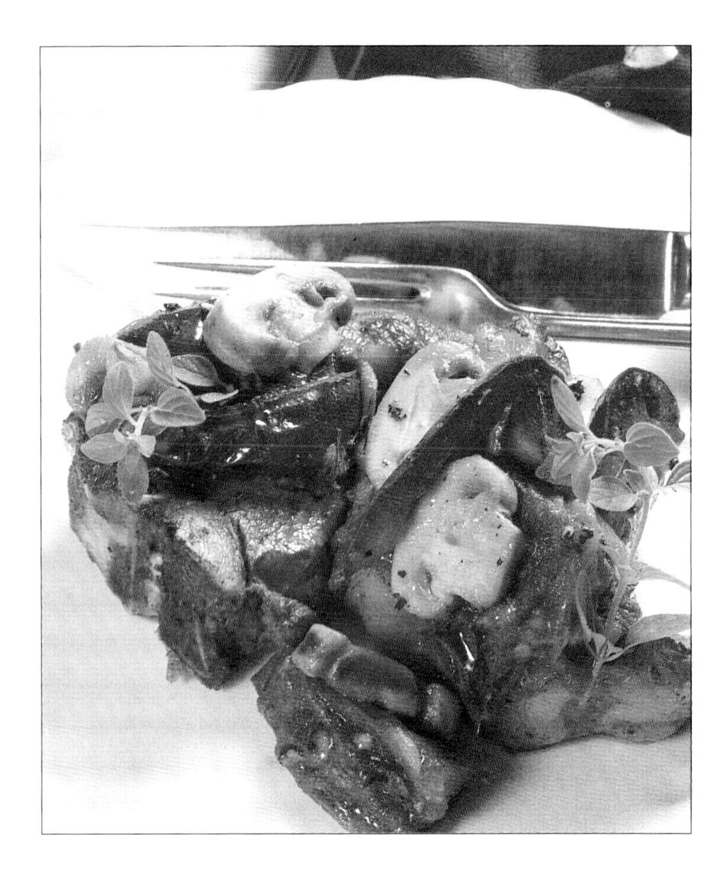

MUSHROOM AND TOMATO-TOPPED CHOPS

4 lamb loin chops, each 2.5 cm (1 inch) thick
15 ml (1 tbsp) lemon juice
milled pepper
7.5 ml (1½ tsp) mustard powder
3 cloves garlic, crushed

TOPPING
2 large ripe tomatoes, or 4 – 6 canned tomatoes
butter and oil for frying
10 button mushrooms, sliced
salt and milled pepper
5 ml (1 tsp) sugar
5 ml (1 tsp) chopped fresh basil
SERVES 4

TOPPING: Slice tomatoes into eighths. Heat butter and oil and sauté tomatoes for 5 minutes. Add remaining topping ingredients, cover and cook until softened. Sprinkle lamb chops with lemon juice, pepper, mustard powder and garlic. Set aside. Meanwhile, heat grill. Place chops in a grill pan and grill, allowing 3 – 4 minutes a side. Serve with tomato and mushroom topping.

COOK'S NOTES
▲ Oregano may be used instead of basil.
▲ Season the fat after cooking is completed.

STICKY LAMB RIBLETS

16 lamb riblets (allow 4 riblets per person)

SAUCE
60 ml (4 tbsp) honey
60 ml (4 tbsp) soy sauce
45 ml (3 tbsp) tomato sauce
60 ml (4 tbsp) orange juice
30 ml (2 tbsp) brown vinegar
30 ml (2 tbsp) white wine
4 cloves garlic, crushed
10 ml (2 tsp) mustard powder
milled pepper
SERVES 4

Preheat oven to 180 °C (350 °F/gas 4). Grill riblets on rack of a grill pan for 5 minutes on each side. Meanwhile, mix all sauce ingredients together. Tip riblets into grill pan (some, but not all, of the lamb fat should be removed). Pour over sauce and cook for 25 minutes, shaking pan once during cooking. Serve with baked potatoes and salad or stir-fried vegetables flavoured with a few sprigs of fresh rosemary.

COOK'S NOTES
▲ Pork spare ribs may be used instead of lamb, but add about 10 minutes to cooking time.
▲ Remove riblets from pan as soon as they are cooked, as they tend to absorb too much fat if they are left to stand.

GAMMON STEAKS WITH SPICED APPLE SALSA

8 gammon steaks (about 575 g/1¼ lb)
2.5 – 5 ml (½ – 1 tsp) mustard powder
milled pepper
butter and oil for frying
125 ml (4 fl oz) cider or apple juice

SALSA
2 Golden Delicious apples, grated
15 ml (1 tbsp) sugar
juice of 1 small lemon or lime
2.5 ml (½ cup) caraway seeds or rosemary leaves
sunflower oil
SERVES 4

Mix salsa ingredients together and, if there's time, set aside for 1 hour to marinate. Season gammon with mustard and pepper and set aside. Heat butter and oil and add gammon. Fry briefly on both sides. Increase the heat, add cider or apple juice and cook for 3 – 5 minutes (cider or apple juice should evaporate slightly). Serve with apple salsa and glazed baby onions and potatoes.

COOK'S NOTES

▲ Gammon steaks are available prepacked from supermarkets. If they are small, you may need more than two per person.

▲ Pork chops, fillet or schnitzel may be used instead of the gammon steaks.

FILLET STEAK WITH MUSTARD BUTTER

4 x 3 cm (1¼ inch) thick slices fillet steak
5 ml (1 tsp) mustard powder
milled pepper
butter and sunflower oil for frying

MUSTARD BUTTER
60 ml (4 tbsp) softened butter
5 ml (1 tsp) mustard powder
10 ml (2 tsp) Dijon mustard
2.5 – 5 ml (½ – 1 tsp) light mustard seeds, heated until popped (optional)
2.5 ml (½ tsp) salt
SERVES 4

Wipe meat with a damp cloth and pat dry. Season with mustard and pepper. Heat butter and oil in a heavy-based frying pan until just smoking. Place steaks in pan and sear each side quickly. Continue cooking for 3 – 4 minutes on each side for a rare steak and an extra 1 – 2 minutes for medium-done. The flavour and texture of fillet is ruined when it is cooked for too long.

MUSTARD BUTTER: Mix all ingredients together and chill until needed. To serve, place a slice on top of each fillet and serve with vegetables, sautéed potatoes and onions.

COOK'S NOTES

▲ It is usually cost effective to buy a whole fillet and cut it into steaks, rather than buy individual steaks.

SOUVLAKI

500 g (18 oz) boneless shoulder or leg of lamb
juice of ½ small lemon
sunflower oil and butter for frying
3 cloves garlic, crushed
10 ml (2 tsp) cumin
5 ml (1 tsp) dried or 15 ml (1 tbsp) chopped fresh oregano
about 60 ml (4 tbsp) white wine
salt and milled pepper
4 pitta breads
diced tomatoes
shredded lettuce
sliced onion
sliced gherkins (optional)
marinated mushrooms (optional)
diced red, green and yellow peppers (optional)
tzatziki (see Cook's Notes)
SERVES 4

Wipe meat with a damp cloth. Cut into 2 cm (¾ inch) cubes and squeeze lemon juice over. Heat butter and oil, add garlic and cumin and sauté for 2 minutes. Add lamb and brown on all sides to seal. Add oregano, wine and seasoning. Cook until soft and still slightly pink in centre. Cut open pitta breads. (Warm slightly in oven first, if desired.) When meat is cooked, pile into pitta bread halves, add vegetables and spoon mounds of garlicky tzatziki over (see Cook's Notes).

COOK'S NOTES

▲ To make tzatziki, mix cottage cheese, grated and drained cucumber, crushed garlic, lemon juice and seasoning.

▲ Garlicky, baby meatballs may be used as a pitta filling instead of lamb.

LAMB CHOPS VINAIGRETTE

8 small lamb cutlets or
4 lamb loin chops
3.75 ml (¾ tsp) mustard powder
milled pepper

VINAIGRETTE
2 cloves garlic, crushed
salt and milled pepper
20 – 30 ml (4 – 6 tsp) chopped fresh rosemary
3.75 – 5 ml (¾ – 1 tsp) wholegrain mustard
3.75 ml (¾ tsp) sugar
60 ml (4 tbsp) balsamic or red wine vinegar
125 ml (4 fl oz) olive or sunflower oil
SERVES 4

Season chops with mustard and pepper. Preheat grill. Grill chops to desired degree, turning once.

VINAIGRETTE: Heat all ingredients together in a small saucepan. Bring to the boil. Reduce heat and simmer for about 2 minutes. Spoon vinaigrette over chops and serve with baby potatoes and crisp steamed vegetables.

COOK'S NOTES

▲ For a mint-flavoured vinaigrette, which will enhance the flavour of the lamb, substitute mint for rosemary, omit garlic and add 2.5 ml (½ tsp) extra sugar.

OLD-FASHIONED LIVER AND ONIONS

- butter and sunflower oil for frying
- 2 medium onions, sliced
- 500 g (18 oz) calf's or lamb's liver, membranes removed and flesh sliced
- 75 ml (5 tbsp) beef stock (made with ¼ beef cube)
- 45 ml (3 tbsp) white wine
- pinch sugar
- salt and milled pepper

SERVES 4

Heat butter and oil in a large frying pan. Sauté onion until beginning to brown. Add liver and stir-fry for about 2 minutes to brown slightly. Add remaining ingredients and cook over high heat for about 5 minutes. The liver should be pink in the centre and springy to the touch. Scrape off any residue left in the pan and serve with liver, noodles and vegetables.

COOK'S NOTES

▲ Add 5 – 7.5 ml (1 – 1 ½ tsp) Dijon mustard, or add both mustard and about 60 ml (4 tbsp) single cream for a richer dish.

▲ Chopped bacon may be added. Fry until crisp, and add at the same time as the onions.

ORIENTAL PORK FILLET

Lean, healthy, ultra-tender – pork fillet is certainly worth a try

- about 575 g (1¼ lb) pork fillet
- juice of 1 orange
- juice of ½ lemon
- 60 ml (4 tbsp) soy sauce
- 30 ml (2 tbsp) olive or sunflower oil
- salt and milled pepper
- 5 ml (1 tsp) each ground coriander and cumin
- 4 cloves garlic, crushed

SERVES 4

Clean fillet with a damp cloth and place in a roasting tin. Mix orange and lemon juice, soy sauce and oil together and brush liberally over meat. Pat fillet with seasoning, spices and garlic. Roast at 180 °C (350 °F/gas 4) for 10 minutes. Baste fillet with orange mixture and continue cooking for a further 10 minutes. Baste once again, roast for a further 5 minutes (for a slightly pink fillet), or for a further 5 – 10 minutes for well done meat). Serve sliced, using any remaining cooking juices as gravy.

COOK'S NOTES

▲ Allow about 200 g (7 oz) pork fillet per person and allow 15 – 20 minutes roasting time for every 500 g (18 oz), plus 15 minutes (medium done) or 25 minutes (well done).

PORK WITH PRUNES

A classic French dish – elegant and simple

butter for frying
8 thin pork chops
flour
300 ml (½ pint) dry white wine
300 ml (½ pint) chicken stock
about 12 large prunes, pitted
salt and milled pepper
2 bay leaves
15 ml (1 tbsp) wholegrain mustard
15 ml (1 tbsp) redcurrant jelly or 5 ml (1 tsp) loganberry jam
SERVES 4

Melt butter. Dip chops in flour and shake gently to remove excess. Brown chops on both sides. Add wine, stock, prunes, seasoning, bay leaves and mustard. Bring to the boil, cover and simmer for about 30 minutes or until chops are tender. Place pork on a serving platter. Bring remaining pan juices to the boil, stir in jelly and continue to boil until slightly reduced. Adjust seasoning and pour over meat. Serve with crunchy steamed vegetables and boiled potatoes.

AVOCADO AND LEMON LIVER

A delicious, make-in-a-minute meal that's packed with nutrients

butter and sunflower oil for frying
2 large onions, thinly sliced
3.75 ml (¾ tsp) sugar
6 – 8 sage leaves (optional)
4 x 250 g (9 oz) slices calf's liver
flour for coating
juice of 1 – 2 lemons
salt and milled pepper
1 – 2 ripe avocados
SERVES 4

Heat butter and oil in a frying pan and sauté onions until glossy but not too brown, about 5 minutes. Add sugar and sage leaves, if using. Stir lightly and move to one side of pan while cooking liver, or remove and keep warm. Lightly coat liver with flour and tap gently to remove any excess. Add liver to pan and, after about 30 seconds, squeeze over liberal quantities of lemon juice. Brown liver lightly on both sides – not more than 2 minutes a side. Place liver on plates with onion mixture, season with salt and milled pepper, and garnish with mashed avocado sprinkled with lemon juice to prevent browning. Serve immediately with sautéed potatoes and a salad.

LAMB CHOPS WITH ORANGE-MUSTARD GLAZE

8 lamb cutlets or 4 large loin chops

ORANGE-MUSTARD GLAZE
juice of 1 small orange
10 ml (2 tsp) lemon juice
5 – 10 ml (1 – 2 tsp) mustard powder
30 ml (2 tbsp) wholegrain mustard
5 ml (1 tsp) brown sugar
SERVES 4

Mix glaze ingredients together well. Wipe chops with a damp cloth. Heat grill. Liberally baste chops, including fat, with orange mixture. Grill for 2 minutes, turn, baste and grill for a further 2 minutes. Baste once more and grill for a further minute (for rare lamb). If fat does not become crisp, insert a skewer through centre of chops, stand fat-side up, baste and grill for about 1 minute. (Watch carefully as fat will burn quite quickly.) Serve with new potatoes and steamed green vegetables.

COOK'S NOTES

▲ Use a tender cut of lamb, as tougher cuts are not suitable for grilling.

▲ Don't salt chops before cooking, as it toughens the meat.

TRICOLOUR PEPPER STEAK

4 x 250 g (9 oz) sirloin steaks
butter and sunflower oil for frying
1 each red, yellow and green pepper, seeded and cut into strips
2 cloves garlic, crushed
5 ml (1 tsp) mustard seeds
30 ml (2 tbsp) white wine
3.75 ml (¾ tsp) sugar
salt and milled pepper
SERVES 4

Wipe steaks with a damp cloth. Set aside. Heat butter and oil and lightly sauté peppers, garlic and mustard seeds for 3 minutes. Add wine and sugar, stir and heat through. Heat butter and oil in another frying pan. Add steak and fry, turning once, until done: 1 – 2 minutes each side for rare; 2 – 3 minutes each side for medium; 4 – 5 minutes each side for well-done. Season with salt and pepper.

COOK'S NOTES

▲ The steak may also be grilled. Timing and method remain the same.

▲ Don't season steak before cooking; too many juices will be lost.

▲ To test if the steak is done to taste, insert a skewer in the thickest part of the meat. Rare steak should be reddish pink; medium slightly pink and well-done should be an even colour throughout.

BARBECUE GAMMON STEAKS

15 ml (1 tbsp) sunflower oil
4 lean gammon steaks
75 ml (5 tbsp) orange juice
75 ml (5 tbsp) tomato sauce
30 ml (2 tbsp) sugar
60 ml (4 tbsp) cider vinegar or white wine vinegar
15 ml (1 tbsp) prepared mustard
15 ml (1 tbsp) Worcestershire sauce
SERVES 4

Heat oil in large frying pan for about 1 minute. Add gammon steaks and cook for 3 minutes on each side, or until browned. In a small bowl, mix remaining ingredients together and add to steaks. Simmer for 8 – 10 minutes. Add some freshly milled pepper and serve with mashed potatoes or crusty bread to mop up sauce.

COOK'S NOTES

▲ Pineapple juice or water may be used instead of orange juice.

▲ White wine may be used instead of the vinegar.

▲ For an extra tang, add a little chilli sauce to the barbecue sauce.

AVOCADO AND GAMMON FRY

Take care not to cook the avocado for too long, as it will get hard and bitter

- 30 ml (2 tbsp) sunflower oil
- 10 ml (2 tsp) butter
- 1 onion, cut into eighths
- 3 slim leeks, sliced into 2 cm (¾ inch) pieces
- about 15 baby new potatoes, halved and parboiled until *al dente*
- 400 g (14 oz) gammon steaks, cubed
- 60 ml (4 tbsp) white wine
- 5 ml (1 tsp) each sugar and mustard powder
- 1 small avocado, cubed
- salt and milled pepper

SERVES 4

Heat oil and butter in a large pan. Add onion and leeks and sauté until golden. Add potatoes and toss to coat in butter. Add meat, brown lightly on both sides and add wine, sugar and mustard. Cook over high heat for about 5 minutes. Add avocado, toss gently to heat through, season and serve immediately.

COOK'S NOTES

▲ Bacon, ham or smoked sausage can replace the gammon steaks.

▲ If you have real German mustard, add 15 ml (1 tbsp) to the dish. It adds a marvellously piquant flavour, but can be expensive and more difficult to find.

GREEK-STYLE MEAT LOAF WITH TZATZIKI

750 g (1¾ lb) lean mince
1 large onion, finely chopped
5 fat cloves garlic, crushed
about 10 green or black olives, coarsely chopped (optional)
1 egg
5 ml (1 tsp) sugar
30 ml (2 tbsp) chopped fresh oregano or 10 ml (2 tsp) dried
1 beef stock cube, crumbled
45 ml (3 tbsp) Worcestershire sauce
5 ml (1 tsp) mustard powder
60 ml (4 tbsp) rolled oats
a little salt
milled pepper
SERVES 4

Mix all ingredients together well and pack into a greased loaf tin. Bake at 180 °C (350 °F/gas 4) for 40 – 45 minutes. Remove from oven, pour off excess fat and allow to rest for about 10 minutes before slicing. Serve with salad and tzatziki.

COOK'S NOTES

▲ Tzatziki: Peel and grate ½ cucumber and drain. Mix with 1 crushed clove garlic, a dash of lemon juice and 175 ml (6 fl oz) thick yoghurt. Season with salt and milled pepper.

ROSEMARY LAMB CHOPS

sunflower oil and butter for frying
2 cloves garlic, thinly sliced
leaves of 1 large sprig rosemary
8 lamb chops
salt
milled pepper
200 ml (7 fl oz) beef stock, made with 1 cube
60 ml (4 tbsp) white wine
5 ml (1 tsp) sugar
SERVES 4

Heat oil and butter, add garlic and half rosemary leaves and sauté for 30 seconds. Add chops and fry on both sides until cooked, about 2½ minutes on each side. Remove and keep warm. Add salt before serving. Turn heat up to high. Pour off any excess oil but don't remove pan scrapings. Add pepper to taste, beef stock, white wine, sugar and remaining rosemary leaves. Cook over high heat, uncovered, until liquid reduces by just over half. Serve sauce separately

COOK'S NOTES

▲ Lamb cutlets, loin or chump chops may be used.

▲ If the fat is not crisp enough but the meat is cooked, hold the meat with a pair of tongs (not a fork) and dip fat directly into hot fat to cook it to desired degree of crispness.

▲ Don't season the meat with salt before cooking it, as this tends to toughen it. Add salt just before serving.

STEAK WITH MUSTARD-GLAZED ONIONS

butter and oil for frying
3 large onions, sliced
4 cloves garlic, sliced
10 – 15 ml (2 – 3 tsp) mustard seeds
1 large sprig fresh rosemary, chopped
15 ml (1 tbsp) wholegrain mustard
salt and milled pepper
45 ml (3 tbsp) port, marsala wine or sherry
milled pepper
mustard powder
4 sirloin or porterhouse steaks
SERVES 4

Heat butter and oil and gently sauté onions, garlic and mustard seeds. When seeds begin to pop, add rosemary and wholegrain mustard. Simmer gently. Meanwhile, heat butter and oil in another pan, season steaks and fry to desired degree of tenderness. Just before steaks are ready, increase heat under simmering onions, season and stir in port. Serve steaks topped with onion mixture and some juices from the steak pan.

MINIATURE ORIENTAL MEATBALLS

450 g (1 lb) minced pork
1 onion, finely chopped
45 ml (3 tbsp) chopped coriander or 5 ml (1 tsp) dried
10 – 15 ml (2 – 3 tsp) chopped fresh ginger
45 ml (3 tbsp) Hoi-sin sauce (see Cook's Notes)
1 large egg
flour for coating
butter and oil for frying

TO SERVE
500 g (18 oz) Chinese noodles
250 – 375 ml (8 – 13 fl oz) chicken stock
thinly sliced spring onions, mangetout, carrots, courgettes
30 ml (2 tbsp) soy sauce
30 ml (2 tbsp) Hoi-sin sauce
SERVES 4

Mix all ingredients, except flour, butter and oil, until blended. Shape into balls and coat with flour. Heat butter and oil in a pan and fry meatballs in batches, turning once (about 8 – 10 minutes). Drain on paper towels and keep warm. Boil noodles in chicken stock until tender. Add vegetables and heat through. Drain noodles, stir in sauces, top with meatballs and serve.

COOK'S NOTES

▲ Hoi-sin sauce, available from Chinese delicatessens, is made from soy flour, red beans, chilli, sugar, salt and spices.

PASTA AL PESTO

Pesto is a Genoese speciality made by blending pounded fresh basil, garlic, olive oil and Parmesan cheese together to form a thick sauce. It is most often served with pasta, but is a good accompaniment to fish or chicken dishes too

500 g (18 oz) pasta of your choice
45 ml (3 tbsp) bottled pesto
60 ml (4 tbsp) single cream
1 clove garlic, crushed
about 60 ml (4 tbsp) freshly grated Parmesan cheese
salt and milled pepper
olive oil
SERVES 4

Cook pasta according to packet instructions. Meanwhile, gently heat pesto, cream, garlic and Parmesan cheese together. Season to taste. Drain pasta well, return to saucepan and toss in olive oil and pesto mixture. Serve with a tomato and mozzarella salad and extra freshly grated Parmesan cheese.

COOK'S NOTES

▲ Allow less pasta – about 300 g (11 oz) – for a dish with more sauce.

▲ Use good quality Italian pasta; it's a little expensive but the taste and texture are worth it!

▲ Use only fresh Parmesan cheese; most delicatessens stock it. Store the cheese in an airtight container in your freezer. It never freezes completely, so it can be used immediately.

ASPARAGUS AND BACON PASTA

300 g (11 oz) asparagus offcuts
250 g (9 oz) pasta shapes
sunflower oil for frying
250 g (9 oz) rindless back bacon, chopped
1 bunch spring onions, chopped
1 bunch chives, chopped
30 g (1 oz) chopped parsley
3 cloves garlic, crushed
juice of 1 lemon
salt and milled pepper
60 ml (4 tbsp) olive oil
60 ml (4 tbsp) sunflower oil
SERVES 6

Wash asparagus and steam until *al dente*, rinse in cold water and chill. Cook pasta according to packet instructions until *al dente*, drain and cool. Heat oil and fry bacon until very crisp. Drain on paper towels and set aside. Toss remaining ingredients with cooked pasta, then stir in asparagus. Sprinkle with bacon just before serving.

COOK'S NOTES

▲ This dish looks especially good served on a bed of lettuce.

▲ Cut calories by grilling the bacon.

COURGETTE AND SHRIMP PASTA

400 – 500 g (14 – 18 oz) angel's hair or other fine pasta
6 – 8 medium courgettes
1 bunch spring onions
15 ml (1 tbsp) butter
2 cloves garlic, chopped
30 ml (2 tbsp) white wine
2.5 ml (½ tsp) sugar
salt and milled pepper
2.5 ml (½ tsp) mustard powder
150 g (5 oz) shelled frozen shrimps, thawed
30 ml (2 tbsp) fresh dill or 15 ml (1 tbsp) dried
olive oil
SERVES 4

Cook pasta according to packet instructions. Drain. Slice courgettes and spring onions lengthways to form thin strips. Melt butter and sauté courgettes, spring onions and garlic for about 2 minutes. Add wine, sugar, seasoning, mustard powder and cook for about 5 minutes. Add shrimps and dill, stir to coat. Cover pan and cook for about 3 minutes. Drizzle drained pasta with a little olive oil, pour over sauce and mix together.

COOK'S NOTES

▲ Thaw frozen shrimps by pouring boiling water over them and drain immediately – do not soak them in the water.

RAVIOLI IN A SAGE BUTTER CREAM

about 750 g (1¾ lb) spinach and ricotta ravioli, frozen
60 – 75 ml (4 – 5 tbsp) butter
20 ml (4 tsp) fresh sage or dill, chopped
100 ml (3½ fl oz) single cream
salt and milled pepper
SERVES 4

Break frozen ravioli sheets into pieces. Cook in boiling water with a little salt and oil added. (It will need about 8 minutes' cooking time.) Meanwhile, heat butter until bubbling, add sage or dill and cook for about 4 minutes. Add cream and seasoning and reduce heat. Drain pasta, pour sauce over and serve immediately. Crusty bread and a salad including lots of tomatoes are the perfect accompaniments.

COOK'S NOTES

▲ If liked, serve with freshly grated Parmesan cheese.

▲ Ricotta and spinach ravioli can be bought at some supermarkets and delicatessens. Do not thaw before cooking.

ROAST TOMATO FUSILLI

Spiral-shaped pasta (fusilli) with garlicky roast tomatoes and black olives – what could be better?

olive oil
12 plum, cherry or English tomatoes
about 15 ml (1 tbsp) sugar
6 cloves garlic, crushed
fresh basil or oregano leaves
salt and milled pepper
500 g (18 oz) fusilli or noodles
12 – 16 black olives
grated Parmesan cheese
SERVES 4

Lightly oil a baking sheet. Preheat oven to 200 °C (400 °F/gas 6). Halve tomatoes lengthways. Top each half with equal quantities of sugar, garlic, herbs and seasoning. Bake until soft and slightly shrivelled, about 10 minutes. Place baking sheet near heat and grill until slightly blackened. Meanwhile, cook pasta according to packet instructions, adding crushed stock cubes of your choice to water for extra flavour. When cooked, drain and toss with olives and tomatoes. Season, drizzle with a little olive oil and serve with grated Parmesan cheese.

COOK'S NOTES

▲ Capers, anchovies and whole roast garlic cloves make wonderful additions to the tomatoes and pasta.

TAGLIATELLE WITH A COOL BASIL AND TOMATO SAUCE

This hot and cold pasta tops the list of trendy taste-tempters

- 8 large, very ripe tomatoes
- 45 g (1½ oz) loosely packed fresh basil leaves
- 2 fat garlic cloves, crushed (optional)
- 5 ml (1 tsp) sugar
- 60 ml (4 tbsp) good quality olive oil
- salt and milled pepper to taste
- 500 g (18 oz) tagliatelle or pasta of your choice
- olive or sunflower oil
- freshly grated Parmesan cheese

SERVES 4

SAUCE: Blanch tomatoes in boiling water for 2 minutes, refresh in cold water and skin. Chop coarsely. Tear basil leaves into small pieces. In a large bowl, mix tomatoes, basil, garlic, sugar, olive oil and seasoning. Set aside.
Cook pasta according to packet instructions. Drain and toss in olive or sunflower oil. Spoon on to piping hot plates and top with basil and tomato sauce. Serve with Parmesan cheese and a green salad.

COOK'S NOTES

▲ The tomato and basil sauce may be prepared a day in advance and refrigerated until needed.
▲ If you can't find fresh basil, use half the quantity of fresh oregano. If all else fails use 1 large bunch of chives, finely chopped, and include the garlic.
▲ Take care not to overcook the pasta; it should be *al dente* – still slightly firm.

SPINACH AND SALMON TROUT PASTA

500 g (18 oz) ribbon noodles
250 – 300 g (9 – 11 oz) spinach, shredded and steamed
45 g (1½ oz) freshly grated Parmesan cheese
60 ml (4 tbsp) olive oil
milled pepper
dill fronds to garnish

SAUCE
about 300 g (11 oz) smoked salmon trout trimmings
4 tomatoes, peeled
2 bunches spring onions, finely chopped
250 ml (8 fl oz) single cream
30 g (1 oz) chopped fresh dill
juice of 1 lemon
2.5 ml (½ tsp) sugar
60 ml (4 tbsp) natural yoghurt
milled pepper
SERVES 4

SAUCE: Finely chop salmon trout. Dice tomatoes, drain and toss with salmon. Stir in remaining ingredients and season to taste. Cook pasta according to packet instructions. Rinse and drain cooked pasta, return to hob and toss with spinach, Parmesan cheese and oil. Season with pepper and serve with sauce at room temperature, garnished with dill.

PASTA ARABBIATA

A traditional Italian pasta gently flavoured with chilli and garlic

4 garlic cloves, thinly sliced
2 – 3 dried chillies, crushed or 5 – 7.5 ml (1 – 1½ tsp) dried chilli flakes
about 100 ml (3½ fl oz) olive oil
500 g (18 oz) spaghetti or pasta of your choice
45 ml (3 tbsp) chopped parsley
SERVES 4

Sauté garlic and chillies in olive oil until garlic is golden. Pour into warmed serving bowl. Cook spaghetti according to packet instructions, until *al dente*. Drain. Add spaghetti and parsley to chilli and garlic. Toss well. Serve immediately with a crusty white loaf and a mixed salad.

COOK'S NOTES

▲ Don't substitute sunflower oil for olive oil; the taste will never be the same.

▲ Fettuccine, spaghettini or even ribbon noodles make excellent alternatives to the spaghetti. Flavoured noodles – spinach, for example – are also good choices.

▲ Basil could be used instead of parsley.

▲ Peel whole cloves of garlic and store them in a jar of oil in the refrigerator. Not only do the cloves keep longer, but they make the most fragrant garlic oil.

SPRING VEGETABLE PASTA

2 – 4 slim leeks
4 – 6 courgettes
2 – 4 carrots
5 spring onions
15 ml (1 tbsp) sunflower oil
10 ml (2 tsp) butter
10 ml (2 tsp) mustard seeds
3 cloves garlic, crushed
5 ml (1 tsp) sugar
30 ml (2 tbsp) white wine
salt and milled pepper
10 ml (2 tsp) mustard powder
30 ml (2 tbsp) finely chopped parsley
30 ml (2 tbsp) fresh basil leaves or 5 ml (1 tsp) dried
7 – 8 chives, left whole, or spring onion greens
500 g (18 oz) pasta of your choice cooked until *al dente*
SERVES 4

Wash and trim leeks, courgettes, carrots and spring onions; slice into thin julienne strips. Heat oil and butter and stir-fry mustard seeds until they begin to pop. Add leeks and carrots and sauté for about 3 minutes. Add garlic, sugar, wine, salt, pepper and mustard powder. Cook over high heat for about 2 minutes. Add courgettes and spring onions and cook until beginning to soften. Add herbs and toss over moderate heat for a few minutes. Toss with drained pasta and a knob of butter. Serve immediately with Parmesan cheese.

SPAGHETTI WITH CORIANDER AND TOMATO

A wonderfully light pasta sauce borrowed from one of my favourite restaurants

6 large, ripe tomatoes, skinned
olive oil for frying
3 cloves garlic
5 ml (1 tsp) sugar
1 chicken or vegetable stock cube
500 g (18 oz) spaghetti
about 60 ml (4 tbsp) olive oil
salt and milled pepper
1 bunch fresh coriander, chopped
SERVES 4

Seed and chop tomatoes. Drain. Heat oil and sauté garlic until glossy. Add tomatoes, sugar and stock cube dissolved in 15 ml (1 tbsp) boiling water. Cook for about 3 minutes. Cook spaghetti according to packet instructions. Rinse, drain and toss in olive oil, salt and pepper. Stir coriander into tomato sauce and cook for 1 – 2 minutes. Toss pasta and sauce together and serve with a crisp salad and freshly grated Parmesan cheese.

COOK'S NOTES

▲ Fresh basil may be used instead of coriander.
▲ For a cheesy pasta, toss about 45 ml (3 tbsp) freshly grated Parmesan into the pasta with the olive oil.

PASTA PEPERONI

If peppers are expensive, use less and add aubergine and extra courgettes

- about 15 ml (1 tbsp) olive oil
- 1 large onion, halved and sliced
- 2 cloves garlic, crushed
- 5 ml (1 tsp) mustard seeds
- 1 each red, yellow and orange peppers, seeded and sliced
- 2 medium courgettes, cut into julienne strips
- salt and milled pepper to taste
- 45 ml (3 tbsp) dry white wine
- 5 – 7.5 ml (1 – 1½ tsp) mustard powder
- ½ chicken stock cube, crumbled
- about 45 ml (3 tbsp) water
- 500 g (18 oz) tagliatelle

SERVES 4

Heat oil and sauté onion and garlic for about 3 minutes. Add mustard seeds and cook for about 2 minutes. Add peppers to pan and sauté for a few minutes. Add remaining ingredients, except pasta, stir and cook just above simmering for about 4 – 5 minutes. Meanwhile, cook pasta according to packet instructions. Rinse with cold water, drain and return to saucepan with a little olive oil. Toss pasta to heat gently, pour over peppers and mix well. Serve immediately with Parmesan cheese and a green salad.

COOK'S NOTES

▲ If you can find a purple Spanish onion, rather use this kind in the pasta sauce. It adds extra colour and flavour.

▲ If orange peppers aren't available, use red and yellow ones only. Green peppers are not suitable.

▲ Don't overcook peppers or courgettes; they should retain their colour and be slightly crunchy.

FRESH VEGETABLE PASTA

The secret of this pasta is adding chopped ripe tomatoes just before serving, allowing them to warm but not cook

olive oil for frying
5 ml (1 tsp) mustard seeds optional
2 medium leeks, well washed and sliced
2 cloves garlic, crushed
2 medium yellow courgettes, sliced
2 medium green courgettes, sliced
3.75 ml (¾ tsp) mustard powder
3.75 ml (¾ tsp) sugar
60 ml (4 tbsp) white wine
60 ml (4 tbsp) chicken or vegetable stock
salt and milled pepper
15 ml (1 tbsp) chopped fresh oregano
500 g (18 oz) pasta of your choice
4 medium ripe tomatoes, coarsely chopped
freshly grated Parmesan cheese
SERVES 4

Heat oil and mustard seeds in a large non-stick pan. When seeds begin to pop, add leeks and sauté until just beginning to soften. Add garlic and courgettes and stir-fry for 2 minutes. Add mustard powder, sugar, wine, stock, seasoning and oregano. Cook pasta according to packet instructions. When vegetables are crisp-tender, stir in chopped tomatoes and cook over high heat until just warmed through, about 2 minutes. Drain pasta and toss with vegetable sauté. Serve immediately with plenty of freshly grated Parmesan cheese.

COOK'S NOTES

▲ Fresh oregano, not dried, must be used. Dried oregano tends to overpower the other flavours in the dish.
▲ It isn't necessary to peel the tomatoes. Because they aren't cooked completely, the skin does not come away from the flesh, and helps to keep them firmer.
▲ If you cannot find yellow courgettes use 4 green ones.
▲ Take care to serve the pasta in heated bowls as the tomatoes cool the dish down faster than usual.

TAGLIATELLE WITH TUNA SAUCE

750 g (1¾ lb) tagliatelle
fresh dill to garnish

SAUCE
40 ml (8 tsp) sunflower oil
200 g (7 oz) canned tuna in oil, drained
4 – 5 anchovy fillets, drained and chopped
10 ml (2 tsp) capers, drained
milled pepper
5 ml (1 tsp) tomato paste
60 ml (4 tbsp) double cream (or more to taste)
SERVES 6

Cover base of a small saucepan with oil. Add tuna, anchovies and capers and season with pepper. Bring mixture to a low simmer, taking care not to boil. Add tomato paste, reduce heat and cook briefly. Set aside in a warm place. Put tagliatelle into a saucepan of fast-boiling, salted water. Cook till pasta is *al dente*. Drain well. Just before serving, add cream to sauce. Serve a portion of pasta in each bowl, and spoon tuna sauce over. Garnish with a sprig of dill or any fresh herb, and serve with a green salad.

COOK'S NOTES

▲ Freshly made tagliatelle is best, but bought can also be used.

▲ Spaghetti may be used if tagliatelle is not available.

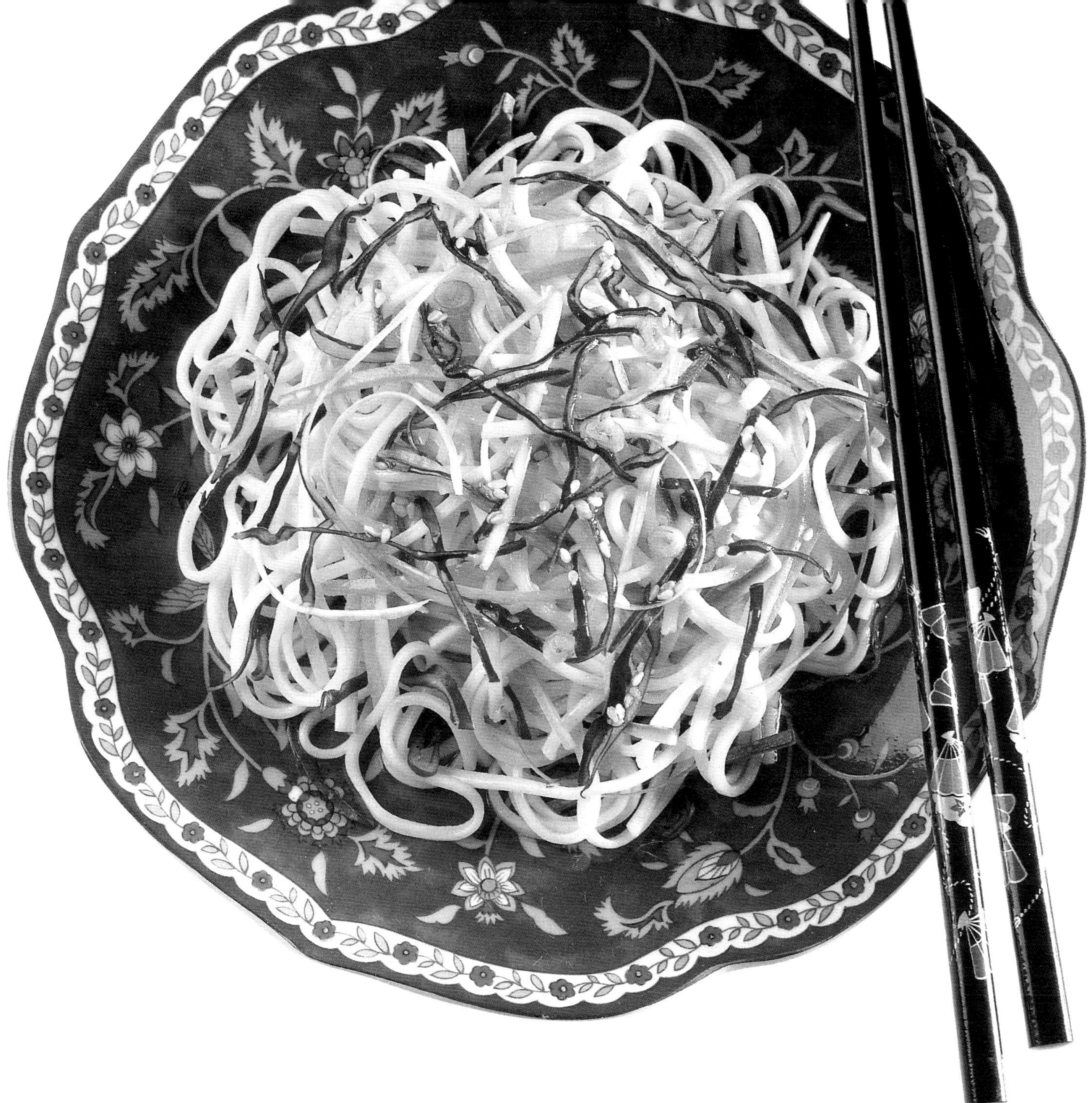

CHINESE NOODLE SALAD

Don't be put off by the number of ingredients in the dressing – it only takes 5 minutes to make and has a delightfully sweet-sour oriental flavour

- about 500 g (18 oz) Chinese noodles or vermicelli
- 8 spring onions, slivered
- 3 – 4 young carrots, cut into matchsticks
- 3 – 4 courgettes, cut into matchsticks

DRESSING
- 20 ml (4 tsp) lemon juice
- 30 ml (2 tbsp) orange juice
- 30 ml (2 tbsp) soy sauce
- 5 ml (1 tsp) peanut or sesame oil
- 60 ml (4 tbsp) olive or sunflower oil
- 1 clove garlic, crushed
- 5 ml (1 tsp) honey or brown sugar
- 10 ml (2 tsp) sesame seeds

SERVES 4

Cook noodles according to packet instructions, rinse with cold water and drain. Toss noodles and vegetables together.
DRESSING: Mix all ingredients together, adjust seasoning according to taste and pour over noodles.

COOK'S NOTES

▲ Bamboo shoots, beansprouts and other vegetables may be added.

▲ Chinese noodles are available at most large supermarkets and delicatessens.

SAUTEED SPINACH AND PARMESAN PASTA

500 g (18 oz) pasta of your choice
8 spring onions, chopped
oil and butter for frying
2 large bunches spinach, stalks removed
45 g (1½ oz) pine kernels, cashew or pecan nuts
salt, milled pepper and sugar to taste
about 30 ml (2 tbsp) olive oil
45 g (1½ oz) freshly grated Parmesan cheese
SERVES 4

Cook pasta according to packet instructions. Meanwhile, sauté spring onions in butter and oil over a low heat. Shred spinach finely, add to spring onions. Increase heat and stir-fry until just cooked. Add nuts. Season with salt, pepper and sugar. (If vegetables or nuts begin to stick, add a dash of white wine to the pan.) Remove spinach mixture from hob. Drain pasta well. Return pasta saucepan to hob, add olive oil and pasta and cook for about 1 minute. Add Parmesan cheese and spinach mixture and toss to mix thoroughly. Serve immediately (otherwise spinach goes black).

COOK'S NOTES

▲ Spaghetti, especially the wholewheat variety, is ideal for this recipe.
▲ The nuts used are quite costly, but the low cost of the pasta makes up for this.
▲ Omit the Parmesan cheese and serve it as a side dish with chicken or fish. Or add 125 g (4 oz) ricotta or cream cheese for a more filling meal.

FALFALLE WITH BLUE CHEESE AND CELERY

Falfalle are pretty bow-shaped noodles. If you can't find them, use noodle shapes of your choice

- butter and sunflower oil for frying
- 1 large onion, chopped
- 1 leek, sliced
- 5 celery stalks, leaves included
- 60 ml (4 tbsp) dry white wine
- 2.5 – 5 ml (½ – 1 tsp) sugar
- 5 ml (1 tsp) mustard powder
- salt and milled pepper
- 400 – 500 g (14 – 18 oz) falfalle
- 150 – 200 g (5 – 7 oz) full cream blue cheese, crumbled
- 125 ml (4 fl oz) single cream (optional)

SERVES 4

Heat butter and oil. Add onion and leek and sauté until glossy. Chop celery, add to pan and sauté for about 2 minutes. Increase heat and add wine, sugar, mustard powder and seasoning. Cover and cook until just soft, about 3 – 5 minutes. Meanwhile, cook pasta according to packet instructions. Drain. Place a knob of butter or a little olive oil in pasta pot and return drained pasta to stove. Pour sauce over, then add blue cheese and cream (if using). Toss to heat pasta, cheese and cream through. Serve with a green salad.

COOK'S NOTES

▲ For a special occasion, add fresh walnuts or pecan nuts to the pasta.

MUSHROOM RAGU WITH POLENTA

MUSHROOM RAGU
butter and sunflower oil
1 large onion, chopped
1 clove garlic, thinly sliced
400 g (14 oz) button mushrooms, thickly sliced
2 large tomatoes, peeled and chopped
1 chicken stock cube, crumbled
30 ml (2 tbsp) white wine
400 g (14 oz) jar or canned tomato passata
3.75 ml (¾ tsp) sugar
salt and milled pepper
15 ml (1 tbsp) chopped fresh basil or oregano

POLENTA
750 ml (1¼ pints) water
125 g (4 oz) coarse ground cornmeal or semolina
30 g (1 oz) butter
60 g (2 oz) grated Parmesan cheese
SERVES 4

RAGU: Heat butter and oil and sauté onion and garlic. Add remaining ingredients, except herbs. Cook for 20 – 25 minutes to obtain a stew-like consistency. Stir in fresh herbs before serving.
POLENTA: Bring water to the boil. Add cornmeal or semolina in a thin stream, stirring to avoid lumps. Stir until polenta begins to come away from sides of saucepan. Stir in butter and Parmesan cheese. Spoon polenta into bowls; top with ragu.

BRAISED VEGETABLES WITH BLUE CHEESE

Serve as a side dish, or with nutty brown rice as a main meal

butter and sunflower oil
1 large onion, peeled and quartered
4 cloves garlic, unpeeled
4 large leeks, well-washed, halved and sliced
2 baby cabbages, quartered
1 large bunch broccoli, broken into florets
about 12 button mushrooms
200 ml (7 fl oz) chicken or vegetable stock, made with 1½ cubes
60 ml (4 tbsp) white wine
3.75 ml (¾ tsp) sugar
5 ml (1 tsp) wholegrain mustard
salt and milled pepper
2 sprigs rosemary
175 – 200 g (6–7 oz) blue cheese
SERVES 4

Heat butter and oil. Break onion into shells and sauté until glossy. Add garlic, leeks and cabbage wedges and stir-fry for 2 minutes. If vegetables stick, add a little stock. Add remaining ingredients, except cheese. Cover and bring to the boil. Reduce heat, remove lid and simmer for about 8 minutes. Remove from heat and crumble cheese over while vegetables are still hot and crisp, or add cheese once vegetables have cooled slightly.

MUSHROOM MEDLEY

Life is not too short to stuff a mushroom, provided that the mushroom is of the large black kind!

butter and sunflower oil for frying
2 medium leeks, well washed and thinly sliced
4 stalks celery with leaves, finely chopped
3 cloves garlic, crushed (optional)
3.75 ml (¾ tsp) sugar
½ vegetable or chicken stock cube, dissolved in
45 ml (3 tbsp) water
30 ml (2 tbsp) white wine
salt and milled pepper
8 large flat mushrooms
100 g (3½ oz) feta cheese, crumbled
½ bunch spring onions, finely chopped
45 ml (3 tbsp) single cream
10 ml (2 tsp) wholegrain mustard
freshly grated Parmesan cheese (optional)
SERVES 4

Heat butter and oil in a large pan and sauté leeks and celery lightly. Add next 5 ingredients and sauté for 2 minutes. Place mushrooms on top and steam, covered for about 5 minutes. Mix remaining ingredients, except Parmesan cheese, and place spoonfuls on top of mushrooms. Sprinkle with Parmesan and grill until cheese has melted and is golden brown.

FRUIT 'N NUT PILAFF

Healthy and filling, this pilaff can be made using pre-cooked rice, sold in chill counters of supermarkets.

250 g (9 oz) cooked mixed brown and wild rice
sunflower oil for frying
1 large onion, chopped
3 large stalks celery (with leaves), chopped
5 ml (1 tsp) each ground cumin and coriander
5 ml (1 tsp) coriander seeds
10 rashers rindless back bacon, chopped
90 g (3 oz) chopped mixed dried fruit
100 g (3½ oz) roughly chopped mixed nuts
45 ml (3 tbsp) sherry
125 ml (4 fl oz) fresh orange juice
½ vegetable stock cube, dissolved in 30 ml (2 tbsp)
boiling water
salt and milled pepper
SERVES 4

Cook rice according to packet instructions, but for 5 – 6 minutes less than specified. Drain. Heat oil and stir-fry onion and celery until glossy. Add spices and cook for 2 minutes. Add bacon and fry for 2 minutes. Add remaining ingredients and simmer for 10 minutes. Toss in rice and cook until heated through.

COCKTAIL POTATO CAKES

3 large potatoes, peeled and parboiled
salt and milled pepper
oil for frying
MAKES 30 MINIATURE POTATO CAKES

Allow potatoes to cool completely (or you can boil them the night before). Grate potatoes coarsely. Season well. Coat pan with oil and heat. Place heaped teaspoonfuls of grated potato in pan and push down gently with a spatula to flatten slightly. Sauté over a moderate heat for 4 – 5 minutes, until bases have crusted and browned. Flip over and sauté for a few minutes more. Place on paper towels to drain, and keep warm. Serve with soured cream, chopped onion and caviare, or dips of your choice.

COOK'S NOTES

▲ If you're worried that the potato cakes will break, add a little beaten egg to the grated potatoes. Don't add too much, as the cakes will fall apart.

WINTER VEGETABLE STIR-FRY

Don't be put off by the long list of ingredients; the recipe is extremely easy

1 onion, sliced
4 cloves garlic, crushed
45 ml (3 tbsp) sunflower oil
1 red, green or yellow pepper, seeded and sliced
3 carrots, sliced
100 g (3½ oz) each broccoli and cauliflower florets
2 courgettes, sliced
1 baby cabbage, finely shredded
60 ml (4 tbsp) soy sauce
30 ml (1 tbsp) Worcestershire sauce
30 ml (1 tbsp) lemon juice
30 ml (1 tbsp) chutney or honey
5 ml (1 tsp) mustard powder
milled pepper
SERVES 4

Using a large frying pan or wok, fry onion and garlic in oil until glossy. Add peppers and carrots and fry, stirring, for 3 – 4 minutes. Add broccoli and cauliflower and cook for a further 4 minutes. Add remaining ingredients and cook for about 4 – 5 minutes. (Vegetables should be crunchy but not raw.) Serve with brown rice or Chinese noodles.

COOK'S NOTES

▲ Nuts or sunflower seeds make a nutritious and crunchy addition.

▲ Most vegetables are suitable for a stir-fry, but remember to use them in an appropriate sequence as some vegetables take longer to cook than others.

▲ Very busy cooks can use packs of ready-chopped vegetables, available from supermarkets, as a base and add any extra vegetables they may have.

▲ Red cabbage adds a wonderful colour to stir-fried vegetables. Shredded spinach also tastes and looks wonderful.

▲ Bacon or diced chicken may be added for extra flavour and bulk.

▲ Try, wherever possible, to use unpeeled vegetables. There's a thin layer just under the skin that contains most of the vitamins and minerals and this is removed with peeling.

MUSHROOM AND POTATO BAKE

Serve with a salad for a filling and nutritious mid-week meal

5 – 6 large potatoes, scrubbed, sliced and parboiled
4 large onions, thinly sliced and parboiled
250 g (9 oz) large flat mushrooms, wiped and sliced
salt and milled pepper
crushed garlic (optional)
250 ml (8 fl oz) soured cream
60 g (2 oz) grated Cheddar, Gruyère or Emmenthal cheese
SERVES 4

Butter an oven-to-table dish. Layer ingredients into dish, first potatoes, then onions and mushrooms. Continue until all have been used, ending with a layer of potatoes. Season soured cream very well and pour over. Sprinkle with grated cheese and bake in a preheated 180 °C (350 °F/gas 4) oven for about 20 minutes or until bubbly and all ingredients are soft. Place under grill for a few minutes to brown cheese.

COOK'S NOTES

▲ Make sure there is enough room in your dish for the extra juice that flows from the mushrooms.

▲ Ordinary cream may be used but don't use yoghurt.

PARTY IDEAS WITH FRESH VEGETABLES AND CHEESE

CUCUMBER SPIRALS
1 cucumber, cut into 1 cm (½ inch) thick slices
feta cheese slices, about 5 mm (¼ inch) thick
milled pepper

CREAM CHEESE AND PEPPER WEDGES
cream cheese or curd cheese
lemon juice
chopped parsley, chives, dill and basil
salt and milled pepper
red, green and yellow peppers, seeded and quartered

CHICORY AND BLUE CHEESE BOATS
chicory or endive
full-cream blue cheese, grated
a little single cream
salt and milled pepper
chopped walnuts or pecan nuts

CUCUMBER SPIRALS: Top cucumber rounds with feta cheese, sprinkle with milled pepper and arrange on a large platter. Ring the changes with Havarti, Port Salut, Brie and Camembert cheese.

CREAM CHEESE AND PEPPER WEDGES: Mix cream cheese, lemon juice, herbs and seasoning together. Fill pepper quarters with cheese mixture and chill until ready to serve. Arrange on a large platter. Other suitable vegetables are button mushroom caps, celery sticks or chicory leaves.

CHICORY AND BLUE CHEESE BOATS: Wash chicory leaves. Mix blue cheese, cream and seasoning together and spoon into leaves. Top with chopped walnuts or pecan nuts.

WARM LEEKS VINAIGRETTE

about 8 leeks

VINAIGRETTE
250 ml (8 fl oz) olive oil
about 60 ml (4 tbsp) white wine vinegar
5 ml (1 tsp) wholegrain mustard
3.75 ml (¾ tsp) mustard powder
5 ml (1 tsp) mayonnaise
3.75 ml (¾ tsp) sugar
salt and milled pepper
Parmesan cheese
SERVES 4 AS A STARTER

Bring a little weak chicken stock to the boil. Add leeks and cook until just soft – about 8 minutes. Meanwhile whisk vinaigrette ingredients, except Parmesan, together. Drain leeks and arrange on individual plates. Pour vinaigrette over still warm leeks. Top with Parmesan shavings or freshly grated Parmesan and serve immediately.

COOK'S NOTES

▲ Green beans, asparagus or artichokes also work well here.

▲ The easiest way to make Parmesan shavings is to use a potato peeler and peel the Parmesan off in shavings. Buying whole chunks of Parmesan is, however, quite expensive, so freshly grated will do just as well.

GARLIC FETA BEANS

Serve the beans on their own with garlic butter as a starter, or top with feta for a more filling first course

about 500 g (18 oz) slender young green beans
60 g (2 oz) butter
3 – 4 cloves garlic, crushed
salt and milled pepper
100 g (3½ oz) feta cheese, sliced
SERVES 4

Fill a saucepan with water, add salt and bring to the boil. Add beans and cook for about 8 minutes, until tender but still crisp. Drain. Melt butter in another saucepan, add garlic and cook for 1 minute. Add beans. Season and toss to coat thoroughly. Spoon onto platter or individual plates, sprinkle with feta and serve immediately.

COOK'S NOTES

▲ Ready-made garlic butter may be used for the beans. Some brands are more potent than others, so buy according to individual taste.

PARTY POTATOES

A quick and stylish way to serve baked potatoes

4 medium baking potatoes
about 250 ml (8 fl oz) soured cream
about 30 g (1 oz) butter
about 200 g (7 oz) smoked salmon off-cuts
1 bunch spring onions, chopped
milled pepper
fresh dill and lemon wedges
SERVES 4

Bake potatoes in an oven or microwave until cooked. Using the oven is the best way to get the skin to crisp. Once cooked, carefully scoop out the pulp, mix all ingredients, except dill and lemon, together. Pile back into potatoes and grill for about 5 minutes. Serve with fresh dill and lemon wedges.

COOK'S NOTES

▲ Smoked salmon trout may be used instead of smoked salmon.
▲ The smoked fish is quite salty so don't add salt to the mixture.
▲ If you can find fresh rocket, it makes an interesting salad to serve with the potatoes.

ASPARAGUS WITH SOURED CREAM AND EGG DRESSING

500 – 575 g (18 oz – 1¼ lb) fresh green asparagus

DRESSING
3 hard-boiled jumbo eggs
1 large onion, very finely chopped
about 15 ml (1 tbsp) capers or pickled gherkins, coarsley chopped
5 ml (1 tsp) tarragon vinegar
5 ml (1 tsp) freshly squeezed lemon juice
125 ml (4 fl oz) soured cream
15 – 30 ml (1 – 2 tbsp) fresh tarragon, parsley or dill, chopped
salt and milled pepper
SERVES 4

Chop eggs finely. Mix with remaining dressing ingredients and refrigerate while cooking asparagus. If you don't have an asparagus steamer, tie asparagus spears with string. Bring an upright saucepan of salted water to the boil. Stand asparagus spears in water, ensuring that tips are out of water. Cover and boil for 4 – 6 minutes, depending on thickness of spears. (This method ensures that stalks cook while tips steam.) Remove asparagus from water, cool slightly and arrange on individual plates. Spoon dressing over and serve, garnished with a lemon wedge, if liked.

THREE-CHEESE POTATOES

4 large potatoes, washed
 and dried
margarine
100 g (3½ oz) blue cheese, grated
100 g (3½ oz) Cheddar cheese,
 grated
100 g (3½ oz) cream cheese
6 – 7 spring onions, chopped
salt and milled pepper
SERVES 4

Rub potatoes with margarine. Place in a cold oven, set temperature to 200 °C (400 °F/gas 6) and bake for 40 – 60 minutes, or until soft inside and crisp outside. Meanwhile, mix cheeses, onions and seasoning together. Remove potatoes from oven, slash open and fill with cheese and onion mixture. (If you have time, remove potato pulp and mix with cheese. Refill potato shells.) Grill for about 3 minutes or until cheese melts. Serve the potatoes with a mixed salad.

COOK'S NOTES

▲ Feta, Emmenthal or Gruyère cheeses make excellent alternatives to Cheddar, blue and cottage cheese.

▲ If you are a garlic fan, crush 2 cloves and add to the potato mixture. For extra colour, add about 30 ml (2 tbsp) chopped chives to the mixture.

MEDITERRANEAN GRILLED VEGETABLES WITH GARLIC AND OREGANO

1 aubergine
3 – 4 courgettes
1 each red, yellow and green pepper
3 leeks
about 125 ml (4 fl oz) olive and sunflower oil, mixed
3 cloves garlic, crushed
salt and milled pepper
1 small bunch fresh oregano
SERVES 4 – 6

Thinly slice aubergine and courgettes horizontally. Remove seeds and membranes from peppers and cut into large flat pieces. Trim leeks and wash thoroughly. Slice lengthways down centre. Mix oil and garlic together and brush over vegetables. Season well. Place vegetables on a baking sheet covered with foil, shiny side up. Scatter oregano leaves over vegetables and add extra oil, if necessary. Grill quite slowly until vegetables are just tender. Increase heat to char edges slightly. Increase heat to char edges slightly. Remove from heat, brush with garlic oil, season and serve at room temperature.

COOK'S NOTES

▲ If your grill doesn't have different temperature settings, start grilling further from heat and then moving baking sheet nearer for charring the vegetables.

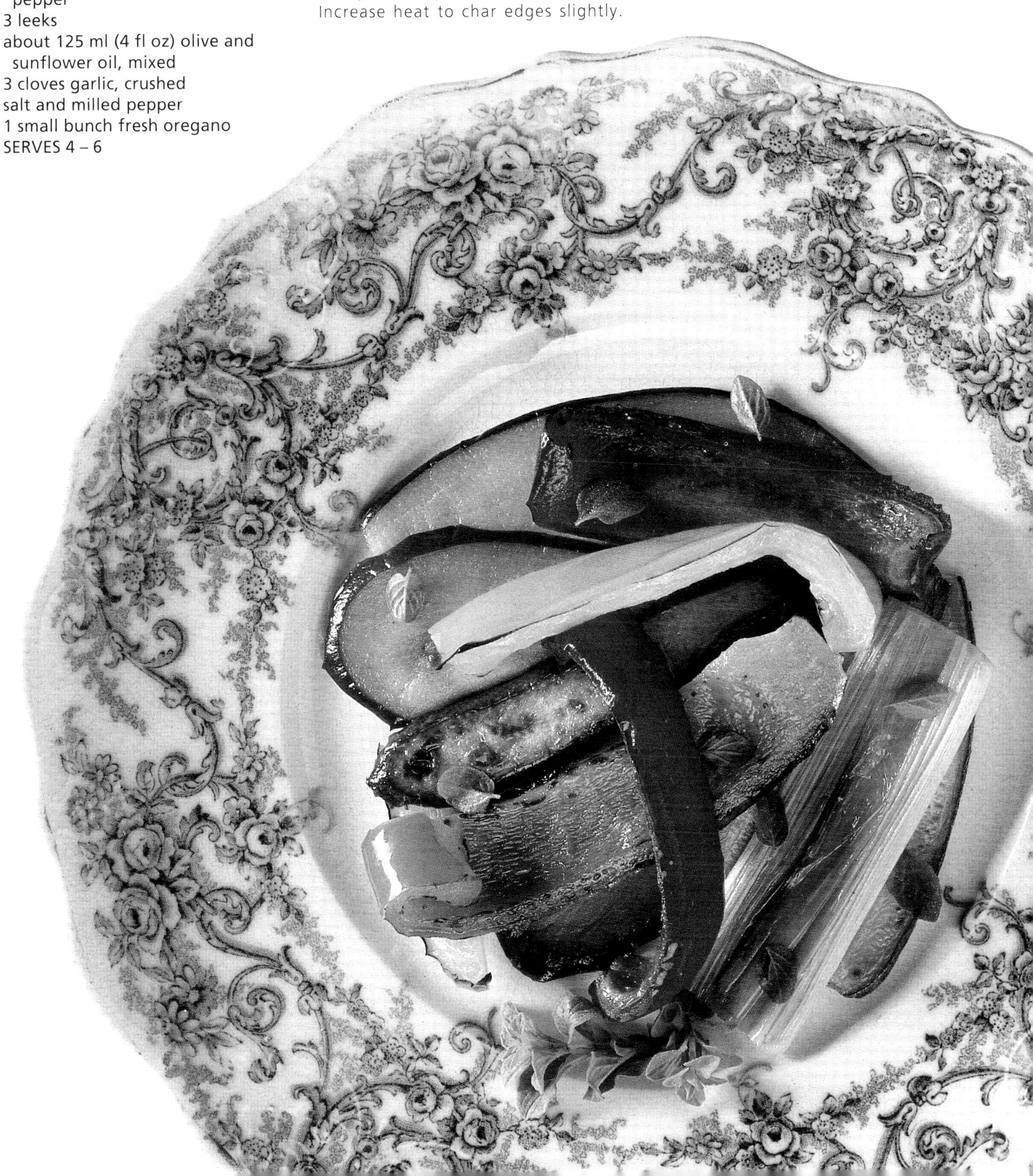

WINTER VEGETABLE VINAIGRETTE

This simple garlicky salad is best served while the vegetables are still warm

200 g (7 oz) each broccoli, cauliflower, green beans and slim leeks, washed
250 – 375 ml (8 – 13 fl oz) chicken or vegetable stock

VINAIGRETTE:
½ each red and yellow peppers, very finely chopped
4 cloves garlic, crushed
15 ml (1 tbsp) chopped capers (optional)
125 ml (4 fl oz) olive oil
about 60 ml (4 tbsp) balsamic, tarragon or white wine vinegar
5 ml (1 tsp) wholegrain mustard
5 ml (1 tsp) mayonnaise
2.5 ml (½ tsp) sugar
10 ml (2 tsp) fresh oregano
salt and milled pepper
SERVES 4

Whisk vinaigrette ingredients together well. Break broccoli and cauliflower into florets. Trim green beans and slice leeks into 4 cm (1½ inch) lengths. Bring stock to the boil, add vegetables and cook until *al dente* (crisp-tender), 5 – 8 minutes. Drain vegetables and arrange on a platter or individual plates. Allow to cool slightly. Pour over dressing and serve with crusty bread to mop up the vinaigrette.

COOK'S NOTES

▲ Do not substitute sunflower oil for olive oil; the flavour will not be the same.

▲ Use your favourite winter vegetables, but do not overcook them; vegetables should be crisp-tender.

▲ For a more filling meal, sprinkle with chopped hard-boiled eggs.

CHINESE SESAME VEGETABLES

A great starter that can just as easily become a filling main course if you add brown rice or noodles. Serve at room temperature

about 300 g (11 oz) sugar snap peas or green beans
about 200 g (7 oz) button mushrooms
3 courgettes, cut into thick strips
12 ears baby corn
3 large carrots, julienned

DRESSING
5 ml (1 tsp) honey
20 ml (4 tsp) soy sauce
60 ml (4 tbsp) vinegar
45 – 60 ml (3 – 4 tbsp) sesame oil
125 ml (4 fl oz) sunflower oil
20 ml (4 tsp) toasted sesame seeds
SERVES 4

Wash vegetables. Top and tail peas. Halve mushrooms. Steam vegetables until *al dente*. Rinse in cold water. Drain and cool. Mix dressing ingredients and drizzle over vegetables just before serving.

COOK'S NOTES

▲ Each vegetable has a different cooking time, so keep a watch to avoid overcooking. The sugar snap peas or beans take the shortest time, followed by the courgettes, mushrooms, carrots and corn.

▲ If you are adding rice or noodles to this dish, you may need to increase the quantity of vegetables.

▲ The dressing will make about 250 ml (8 fl oz). Halve the recipe or refrigerate the excess for up to 1 week. It isn't necessary to double the dressing if you decide to add rice or noodles.

NEW WAVE RICE PUDDING

Rice pudding, the ultimate comfort food, usually takes forever to cook. We've come up with a new version that's still big on comfort but short on time

200 g (7 oz) short-grain white rice
375 ml (13 fl oz) milk
250 ml (8 fl oz) evaporated milk
125 – 175 g (4 – 6 oz) sugar
200 ml (7 fl oz) single cream
grated nutmeg to taste
SERVES 4

Place rice in a large saucepan with milk and evaporated milk. Bring to the boil, stirring occasionally. Reduce heat and simmer, stirring from time to time, until almost all the milk is absorbed. Stir in sugar, cream and nutmeg and simmer, stirring constantly, until thickened. Pour mixture into a serving dish or individual ramekins, sprinkle with more nutmeg and place under a hot grill for a minute or two. Serve hot.

COOK'S NOTES

▲ The milk forms a skin during boiling; remove this.

▲ For very soft rice, add extra milk and simmer slowly until it is all absorbed.

CARAMELIZED ORANGES

3 – 4 oranges
30 g (1 oz) butter
15 ml (1 tbsp) honey or brown sugar
15 ml (1 tbsp) orange liqueur or brandy
juice of ½ small lemon
5 ml (1 tsp) finely chopped preserved ginger (optional)
brown sugar
SERVES 4

Peel oranges, removing all pith. Slice into 5 mm (¼ inch) rounds. Melt butter in a large frying pan. Add honey or sugar and orange slices and cook for 2 – 3 minutes. Add liqueur, lemon juice and ginger and cook until oranges are soft. Transfer oranges to a baking sheet and sprinkle a thin layer of brown sugar over each slice. Grill until sugar melts. Reduce sauce in pan by boiling vigorously, uncovered, for a few minutes. Pour over caramelized oranges and serve immediately with lightly whipped cream or a mixture of honey and natural yoghurt.

COOK'S NOTES

▲ Sliced pineapple may be used instead of oranges, but then substitute rum for the orange liqueur.

▲ Fresh ginger, peeled and very finely sliced, may be used instead of preserved ginger.

PEACHES WITH MASCARPONE

4 cling peaches
500 ml (17 fl oz) water
225 g (8 oz) sugar
2.5 ml (½ tsp) each vanilla and almond essence
30 ml (2 tbsp) lemon juice
1 cinnamon stick
about 125 g (4 oz) mascarpone or cream cheese
60 ml (4 tbsp) honey, melted
45 ml (3 tbsp) toasted flaked almonds
SERVES 4

Wash peaches well and peel. Bring water, sugar, essences, lemon juice and cinnamon stick to the boil. Poach peaches for 3 – 4 minutes, or until just soft. Remove and cool. Halve peaches and remove stones. Beat cheese and melted honey together and spoon into centre of each peach half. Chill. Sprinkle with toasted almonds before serving.

COOK'S NOTES

▲ Canned cling peach halves may be used instead of fresh peaches. Omit poaching stage.
▲ Mascarpone is available from most supermarkets.

FRESH FRUIT CREAMS

200 ml (7 fl oz) double or whipping cream
200 ml (7 fl oz) natural yoghurt
30 ml (2 tbsp) caster sugar or honey
45 ml (3 tbsp) almond liqueur or 2.5 ml (½ tsp) almond essence
150 g (5 oz) chopped fresh fruit of your choice
45 ml (3 tbsp) toasted almonds, wafers, or sliced fresh fruit to decorate
SERVES 4

Mix all ingredients together. (You may need a dash of lemon juice.) Sprinkle with nuts or decorate with wafers or sliced fresh fruit, and serve.

COOK'S NOTES

▲ Any soft fruits may be used. It may be a good idea to use a variety of complementary leftovers.
▲ If you don't like almonds, try to match the liqueur or essence with the fruit you are using.

BOOZY CHERRIES

2 x 400 g (14 oz) pitted cherries
125 g (4 oz) sugar
2.5 ml (½ tsp) ground cinnamon
250 ml (8 fl oz) dry red wine
22.5 ml (4½ tsp) cornflour
150 – 175 ml (5 – 6 fl oz) double cream, whipped
SERVES 6

Drain cherries and set aside. Place sugar, cinnamon and red wine in a saucepan. Bring to the boil and simmer for 5 minutes. Slake cornflour with a little juice and stir into syrup to thicken slightly. Simmer for 5 minutes. Pour into a bowl and chill. Add cherries. Stir half the cream lightly into the cherry sauce and top with remaining cream.

COOK'S NOTES

▲ The dessert may also be served warm, with cream or ice cream.

▲ Stir a dash of brandy into the sauce for extra flavour.

HONEYED APPLE CRÊPES

3 large apples, peeled and cut into wedges
90 g (3 oz) seedless raisins
75 ml (5 tbsp) apple juice or Calvados
about 125 ml (4 fl oz) water
60 ml (4 tbsp) honey
juice of ½ lemon
5 ml (1 tsp) ground cinnamon
4 crêpes
SERVES 4

Place all ingredients, except crêpes, in a saucepan. Bring to the boil, cover and simmer until apple wedges are soft. Check sauce and sweeten with more honey to taste, if desired. Heat store-bought crêpes in a pan or make your own. Fill each crêpe with the apple and raisin mixture, then fold and serve with the remaining sauce spooned over.

COOK'S NOTES

▲ Canned pie apples or pears may be used instead of fresh apples.

▲ Crêpes can now be bought vacuum-packed at most supermarkets.

OLD-FASHIONED BAKED APPLES

Pop these apples in the oven when baking something else – they don't need watching and you'll save on fuel

- 4 Granny Smith apples
- 60 g (2 oz) butter
- 100 g (3½ oz) seedless raisins
- 10 ml (2 tsp) ground cinnamon
- 5 ml (1 tsp) mixed spice
- juice of 1 small lemon
- 60 ml (4 tbsp) honey or brown sugar
- 125 ml (4 fl oz) orange or apricot juice

SERVES 4

Core apples but don't cut right through (otherwise stuffing will fall out). About 2 cm (¾ inch) down from top of each apple, make a slit around circumference to prevent apples bursting during cooking. Mix remaining ingredients, except fruit juice, in a bowl. Press stuffing mixture into each apple. Place in an ovenproof dish, pour over fruit juice and bake in a preheated 180 °C (350 °F/gas 4) oven for 35 – 40 minutes.

COOK'S NOTES

▲ Cooking time will vary according to the size and ripeness of the apples. To check if cooked insert a skewer into each apple; the skin should be quite tough and the flesh should be soft.

▲ Nuts, preferably almonds, can be added to the apple stuffing for a wonderful crunchy texture and a fuller flavour.

▲ Adding a little brandy or liqueur to the fruit juice will make this a star dessert.

CHOCOLATE-DIPPED FRUIT

100 g (3½ oz) plain chocolate
100 g (3½ oz) milk chocolate
100 ml (3½ fl oz) single cream
60 ml (4 tbsp) brandy or liqueur of your choice
prepared selected fruits, such as strawberries, grapes, peaches, cherries or melon
SERVES 4

Melt chocolate in a double boiler over simmering water. Stir in the cream and brandy and keep warm. Arrange fruits on a large platter, place chocolate dip in the centre and serve with skewers.

COOK'S NOTES

▲ If you use liqueur, choose one that is compatible with the fruit, an orange-flavoured one, for instance.
▲ Use the real thing for the chocolate dip; cooking chocolate just doesn't have the flavour.

BERRY AND ORANGE CRÊPES

4 crêpes or thin pancakes
60 ml (4 tbsp) butter
45 ml (3 tbsp) fruit-based liqueur
15 ml (1 tbsp) honey
about 16 strawberries, washed and thickly sliced
about 16 tayberries, washed
peeled segments of 1 – 2 oranges (optional)
icing sugar
SERVES 4

Preheat oven to 140 °C (275 °F/gas 1). Heat crêpes in oven for 5 – 6 minutes. In a small saucepan, heat butter, liqueur and honey. Place the crêpes on heated plates, pour over liqueur sauce and top with the berries and oranges. Sprinkle liberally with icing sugar and serve immediately.

COOK'S NOTES

▲ The berries and oranges may also be heated. Simply add them to the butter/liqueur sauce for a few minutes to heat through.
▲ All large supermarkets are now selling ready-made crêpes but cooking instructions differ, so check carefully.
▲ Brandy may be used instead of the liqueur.
▲ Any soft fruit, including canned berries, may be used.

BLUE CHEESE AND PORT

This wonderful standby dessert combines the cheese and dessert course. All the ingredients can be bought at the last minute and the result is the last word in chic dining

125 g (4 oz) creamy blue cheese or Gorgonzola
45 ml (3 tbsp) port or sweet dessert wine
water biscuits
fresh or preserved fruits
SERVES 4

Mash the cheese and port together, adding extra port to taste. Pile in a pretty bowl, surrounded by water biscuits and your choice of fresh or preserved fruits.

COOK'S NOTES

▲ Use a soft, creamy blue cheese, not a Roquefort type.
▲ Port, dessert wine or marsala may be used.
▲ If you have the time and the money, prick a few soft fresh fruits (peaches, grapes, figs and apricots), soak them in dessert wine and serve with the cheese.

PLUMS IN RED WINE

16 ripe plums, washed
45 ml (3 tbsp) sugar
15 – 30 ml (1 – 2 tbsp) water
60 ml (4 tbsp) red wine
thin strip lemon rind
SERVES 4

Place plums in a saucepan and sprinkle with sugar and water. Simmer until sugar dissolves. Add wine and lemon rind. Increase heat slightly and simmer until softened, approximately 10 minutes. Taste and add extra sugar if desired. Spoon over your favourite vanilla ice cream.

COOK'S NOTES

▲ Larger quantities of stewed plums may be made and frozen for later use. Remember to chill thoroughly before freezing.

SESAME-COATED CAMEMBERT WITH PRESERVED FRUITS

Marvellous for lazy cooks, this recipe combines the cheese and dessert courses

500 g (18 oz) Camembert round
1 large egg, lightly beaten
sesame seeds to coat
preserved fruits of your choice
SERVES 4 – 6

Lightly brush cheese with beaten egg. Sprinkle liberally with sesame seeds and shake gently to remove excess seeds. Bake in a preheated 200 °C (400 °F/gas 6) oven for about 8 – 10 minutes. (Centre should be runny and warm.) If sesame seeds are not browned sufficiently, pop cheese under a hot grill for about 1 minute, but take care that it does not overcook and burst. Serve the Camembert on a large platter with water biscuits and preserved fruits.

COOK'S NOTES

▲ Chopped nuts of your choice can replace the sesame seeds for a crunchy outer layer, or both can be omitted.

ITALIAN-STYLE STRAWBERRIES

Vinegar is wonderful with any berries as it brings out their flavour. The best is balsamic vinegar, as it's quite sweet, but it's also expensive, so use whatever you have. Vary quantity of vinegar and sugar according to taste

- about 750 g (1¾ lb) fresh strawberries, washed and hulled
- about 30 ml (2 tbsp) caster sugar
- about 15 – 20 ml (3 – 4 tsp) vinegar

SERVES 4

Place about 10 strawberries in a large bowl, add sugar and vinegar and stir to dissolve sugar. (Don't worry if some strawberries become mushy.) Add remaining strawberries and toss to cover in juice. Add more sugar and vinegar, according to taste. Serve plain or with ice cream, sorbet, cream or a mixture of natural yoghurt and cream.

APRICOT AND GINGER ICE CREAM

- 400 g (14 oz) canned apricots in natural juice, drained
- juice of ½ lemon
- 15 – 20 ml (3 – 4 tsp) chopped preserved or glacé ginger
- 500 ml (17 fl oz) vanilla ice cream

SERVES 6

Purée apricots and stir in lemon juice and ginger. Soften ice cream. Stir in apricot mixture, blending well. Refreeze until set. Serve with brandy snaps or wafers and drizzle a dash of liqueur over.

COOK'S NOTES

▲ Fresh apricots may be used. Cook them in apricot juice, remove skins and purée.

POACHED DRIED FIGS WITH BRANDY SYRUP

350 g (12 oz) dried figs

SYRUP
225 g (8 oz) sugar
500 ml (17 fl oz) water
rind of 1 orange, cut into thin strips
1 cinnamon stick
125 ml (4 fl oz) brandy
SERVES 6

Cut stalks off figs. Dissolve sugar in water over medium heat, then add orange rind, cinnamon stick and brandy. Add figs and simmer gently for about 15 minutes. Remove from heat and allow to cool. Place figs in deep dessert dishes, pour over a little syrup and decorate with orange rind. Serve with whipped cream.

COOK'S NOTES

▲ Serve with thick natural yoghurt instead of cream.

▲ A zester makes cutting orange rind very much easier.

▲ Fresh figs may be poached and served in the same way.

PAPAYA AND NUT ICE CREAM

Nuts add a piquant touch to this dessert

150 g (5 oz) diced papaya, banana or mango
100 g (3½ oz) nuts, chopped
15 ml (1 tbsp) chunky peanut butter
30 ml (2 tbsp) almond liqueur (optional)
100 g (3½ oz) canned granadilla pulp or the pulp of 4 granadillas
750 ml (1¼ pints) vanilla ice cream, softened
SERVES 6

Mix all ingredients together, except for ice cream. Stir fruit and nut mixture carefully into softened ice cream. Place in a bowl and freeze until firm. Serve with wafers and sliced papaya or mango, or with heart-shaped almond cookies.

COOK'S NOTES

▲ Ripe bananas or mango may be used instead of papaya.

▲ Remember that the ice cream needs time to freeze, so make it a few hours, or preferably 1 – 2 days, in advance. If you choose the latter route, remove it from the freezer about 10 minutes before serving to allow it to soften slightly.

POACHED GUAVAS WITH FRESH LEMON CREAM

Poached guavas, without the lemon cream, are perfect for breakfast

8 fresh guavas, peeled
500 ml (17 fl oz) unsweetened guava juice
juice of ½ small lemon
mint or lemon verbena to decorate

LEMON CREAM
200 ml (7 fl oz) double cream
30 ml (2 tbsp) honey
grated rind of 1 lemon
SERVES 4

FRESH LEMON CREAM: Mix cream and honey together, whip until fairly stiff and stir in lemon peel.

Place whole guavas in combined guava and lemon juice and bring to the boil. Reduce heat and simmer very gently until soft. Remove from heat and allow to cool. Place 2 guavas in each dish, add a dollop of lemon cream, a sprig of fresh mint or lemon verbena and serve.

COOK'S NOTES

▲ Sugar may be added to the guava syrup, if desired.

▲ If you have the time, make strips of lemon rind using a zester and sprinkle on top of the dessert.

▲ Thick Greek yoghurt or half cream, half yoghurt may be used to make the fresh lemon cream.

EMERGENCY POACHED GOOSEBERRIES

This refreshing, simple to make, standby dessert can be kept in the refrigerator for up to a week

300 g (11 oz) fresh or canned gooseberries
125 ml (4 fl oz) white wine
30 ml (2 tbsp) medium–cream sherry (optional)
60 ml (4 tbsp) water
30 – 60 ml (2 – 4 tbsp) honey
rind of 1 lemon
3 cardamom pods
SERVES 4

Wash and drain fresh gooseberries or drain canned gooseberries. Set aside. Place remaining ingredients in a saucepan and slowly bring to the boil. Boil vigorously for about 3 minutes and add gooseberries. Reduce heat and simmer until just softening, 2 – 3 minutes (do not allow to burst). Remove from hob. Serve hot or cold with slices of cheesecake, moist chocolate cake or on their own with a mixed cream and yoghurt topping (sweetened, if liked).

FESTIVE CASSATA

500 ml (17 fl oz) vanilla ice cream
100 ml (3½ fl oz) double cream
90 g (3 oz) chopped glacé fruits
60 g (2 oz) chopped nuts or nibbed almonds
45 – 60 ml (3 – 4 tbsp) liqueur or brandy
45 g (1½ oz) plain chocolate, chopped
mint leaves or extra chopped glacé fruit
SERVES 4 – 6

Beat ice cream and cream together. Stir in remaining ingredients, except mint. Spoon into a 23 x 13 cm (9 x 5 inch) lined loaf tin, cover with cling film and freeze. Remove from freezer about 10 minutes before serving. Turn out on to a platter, decorate with mint leaves or chopped glacé fruit, and serve.

COOK'S NOTES

▲ Opt for a creamy, but not too sweet, vanilla ice cream, as the fruit and nut mixture is quite sweet.

SPICY SAUTEED BANANAS

30 – 45 g (1 – 1½ oz) butter
4 bananas
juice of ½ medium lemon
30 ml (2 tbsp) brandy (optional)
about 30 ml (2 tbsp) brown sugar
5 ml (1 tsp) ground cinnamon
SERVES 4

Melt butter in a large non-stick frying pan. Slice bananas lengthways and place in pan. Squeeze over lemon juice, add brandy, sugar and cinnamon and sauté for about 5 – 7 minutes. (Bananas should be tender but still firm.) Transfer to heated plates. Spoon sauce over and serve immediately with cream. For a more filling dessert, buy or make four crêpes, and wrap around bananas. Top with the sauce and a little brandy or liqueur and serve with pouring cream.

COOK'S NOTES

▲ Be daring and add a dash of brandy to the cream served with the bananas.

MERINGUE BASKETS FILLED WITH CREAMY FRUIT PURÉE

Buy these meringue baskets from large supermarkets or, if you're brave enough and have the time, make your own

250 g (9 oz) strawberries
¼ papaya, peeled and seeded
30 ml (2 tbsp) natural yoghurt
30 ml (2 tbsp) cream cheese
10 – 20 ml (2 – 4 tsp) honey
15 – 30 ml (1 – 2 tbsp) rum (optional)
4 meringue baskets
SERVES 4

Purée strawberries, reserving 4 whole fruit for decoration. Purée papaya and stir into strawberry purée. Stir in yoghurt, cheese, honey and rum. Just before serving, fill each meringue basket with purée and decorate with strawberries, and other fruit or berries if liked.

COOK'S NOTES

▲ Any soft berry fruit may be used in place of the strawberries.
▲ Cream may be used instead of yoghurt.
▲ A strawberry liqueur may be substituted for rum, if liked.

BOOZY STRAWBERRIES

200 ml (7 fl oz) fresh orange juice
45 – 60 ml (3 – 4 tbsp) Cointreau
7.5 ml (1½ tsp) brown sugar
1 cinnamon stick
500 g (18 oz) strawberries, washed and hulled
double cream or mascarpone cheese
finely sliced rind of 1 orange for decoration
Italian wafers
SERVES 4

Bring orange juice, liqueur, sugar and cinnamon stick to the boil. Reduce heat and add strawberries. Simmer for 3 – 4 minutes. Remove cinnamon stick. Serve strawberries and syrup hot or cold with double cream or mascarpone cheese mixed with a little honey. Decorate strawberries with slivers of orange rind and two wafers per serving.

COOK'S NOTES

▲ Any soft berry fruit may be cooked this way. Take care not to overcook them, however, as they will turn to mush. Cape gooseberries in particular need no more than 2 minutes' cooking.
▲ Cointreau provides the best flavour, but it is very expensive. Use any orange-flavoured liqueur.
▲ White wine may be used instead of liqueur, but extra sugar will probably be needed. Add about 10 ml (2 tsp).

JANUARY CHRISTMAS PUDDING

Christmas cake and pudding seem to last forever but the trouble is that, by January, they just don't have the same appeal. Avoid waste by trying our new-look Christmas pudding

juice of 1 small orange
juice of ½ lemon
5 ml (1 tsp) ground cinnamon
15 ml (1 tbsp) brandy, orange liqueur or nut liqueur
3 large slices Christmas cake or Christmas pudding
200 g (7 oz) curd cheese
125 ml (4 fl oz) thick natural yoghurt
10 ml (2 tsp) honey
SERVES 4

In a small saucepan gently heat fruit juices, cinnamon and brandy or liqueur. Pour warm liquid over cake or pudding and allow to stand for a few minutes. Meanwhile stir cheese, yoghurt and honey together. Either layer cake and yoghurt mixture in tall parfait glasses or serve in individual ramekins. If you choose one of these options, use cake as a base, top with yoghurt mixture and sprinkle with cinnamon and thin strips of lemon rind.

COOK'S NOTES

▲ Nuts add extra crunch.

▲ Whipped or thick cream may be used instead of curd cheese.

▲ Mascarpone cheese, although very costly, also makes a delicious topping. Mix it with yoghurt.

GRILLED MIXED FRUIT KEBABS

12 strawberries, washed and hulled
1 pineapple, sliced and cubed
2 bananas, cut into 2 cm (¾ inch) thick slices
12 cubes sweet melon
12 dried apricots soaked in orange juice
ginger syrup or honey to baste
icing sugar
mint
SERVES 4

Thread 3 pieces of each fruit onto each of the 4 skewers. Place in a shallow dish. Pour over juice. Preheat grill. Grill fruit kebabs until slightly browned and softened. Place on a plate, sprinkle with icing sugar and decorate with fresh mint.

COOK'S NOTES

▲ If strawberries are not available, use firm green grapes or sliced kiwi fruit.
▲ Alternate the fruit in the kebabs depending on your taste and the season.
▲ Adding a splash of liqueur to the orange juice will give an extra zing.

CHEAT'S PEACH CRUMBLE

4 ripe peaches, blanched and refreshed
60 ml (4 tbsp) rolled oats
60 ml (4 tbsp) desiccated coconut
10 – 15 ginger biscuits, crumbled
juice of ½ lemon
15 ml (1 tbsp) brown sugar
30 g (1 oz) butter
SERVES 4

Cut peaches in half, stone and peel. Place, cut side up, in a baking dish and preheat grill. Mix remaining ingredients together. Spoon some crumble mixture into hollows of peaches. Sprinkle with a little brown sugar and grill until crumble is golden. Serve with whipped cream or natural yoghurt; decorate with mint leaves.

COOK'S NOTES

▲ If you can't find fresh peaches, use peaches canned in syrup or fruit juice.
▲ Sesame, sunflower and poppy seeds all add a delicious flavour to the crumble.

CHOCOLATE ISLANDS

The chocolate discs look terribly impressive but take only minutes to prepare. If time is short, make them a day in advance and refrigerate until needed

200 g (7 oz) plain or milk chocolate
about 500 ml (17 fl oz) each coffee and nut ice cream
cocoa for sifting
SERVES 4

Melt the chocolate over simmering water in a double boiler. Lay a sheet of waxed paper on a work surface. Using a teaspoon, spoon a blob of melted chocolate on to the paper and, using a spatula or teaspoon, spread it out to form a circle 7.5 cm (3 inches) in diameter. It does not have to look perfect. Repeat procedure to make 4 discs or islands. With remaining chocolate, make 8 small (2 cm/¾ inch diameter) discs. Refrigerate until hard, about 5 minutes. Pull paper away and place in a container until ready to use. (They must be refrigerated.) To assemble, place 1 disc on each dessert plate (a large side plate or fish plate is perfect). Spoon an oval shape of each flavour of ice cream on to each disc. Stud ice cream with small discs. (Handle discs as little as possible, as the heat from your hands will make them melt!) Lightly sift cocoa powder over dessert, including plate, and serve immediately.

COOK'S NOTES

▲ Any flavour of ice cream may be used, but chocolate ice cream would make the dish a little too rich.

ORANGES AND GRAPEFRUIT WITH CARAMEL SAUCE

4 oranges
2 pink grapefruit
30 – 45 ml (2 – 3 tbsp) orange liqueur

SAUCE
200 g (7 oz) sugar
125 ml (4 fl oz) water
2.5 ml (½ tsp) cream of tartar
SERVES 6

Peel 1 orange very thinly and remove pith. Slice rind carefully into long, thin strips. Blanch briefly in boiling water, strain and set aside. Peel fruit and slice thinly. Arrange in overlapping slices of different colours in a pretty serving dish. Pour over liqueur and chill.

SAUCE: Just before serving, bring sugar, water and cream of tartar to the boil, stirring until sugar dissolves. Add blanched rind and boil without stirring, until syrup becomes golden. Pour syrup over chilled fruit and serve immediately.

COOK'S NOTES

▲ Ice cream is a wonderful foil for the tartness of crisp oranges and grapefruit.

▲ For a quick and absolutely heavenly shortcut, arrange oranges and grapefruit on a platter, drizzle with a little orange liqueur, and chill. Meanwhile, heat 225 g (8 oz) white sugar in a pot; once it melts, it will turn brown and begin to bubble. Remove from heat and immediately pour over fruit – it will set to a hard, slightly burnt flavoured toffee – delicious!

ISRAELI BREAD AND BUTTER PUDDING

butter for spreading
6 slices raisin kitka or other egg bread, crusts removed
250 ml (8 fl oz) milk
125 ml (4 fl oz) single cream
2 large eggs
1 egg yolk
45 ml (3 tbsp) whisky or brandy
75 g (2½ oz) sugar
3.75 ml (¾ tsp) vanilla essence
SERVES 4

Butter bread on both sides. Set aside. Whisk remaining ingredients together. Layer bread in a buttered oven-to-table dish. (Bread should not come higher than about 3 cm (1¼ inches) below rim of dish.) Pour egg and milk mixture over. Stop adding liquid when no more can be absorbed. Fill a large roasting tin to ¾ full with water, place dish in water and bake at 180 °C (350 °F/ gas 4) for 30 – 35 minutes, or until just set and golden in colour. (Baking in a bain marie ensures even, slow cooking.) Allow to cool slightly before serving with custard, cream or brandy sauce.

COOK'S NOTES

▲ If the kitka doesn't have enough raisins, sprinkle about 45 g (1½ oz) extra in between the layers of bread.
▲ For a spicy touch, add 10 ml (2 tsp) ground cinnamon to the egg mixture.

MINIATURE WAFFLES WITH MARINATED ORANGES

Miniature waffles are available from delicatessens; the oranges may be prepared 2 – 3 days in advance – what could be easier?

250 ml (8 fl oz) water
450 g (1 lb) sugar
125 – 200 ml (4 – 7 fl oz) pure orange juice
1 stick cinnamon
thinly sliced rind of 1 orange
4 oranges, peeled and sliced
8 miniature waffles
grated plain chocolate
orange liqueur (optional)
mint sprigs to decorate
SERVES 4

Bring water, sugar, orange juice, cinnamon and orange peel to the boil. Reduce heat slightly and boil until a thickish syrup forms. Add orange slices and boil for about 5 minutes. Toast waffles according to packet instructions. Serve waffles with oranges, orange syrup, grated chocolate and a sprinkling of liqueur. Decorate with mint leaves and orange strips.

COOK'S NOTES

▲ Ordinary waffles, found in the chill counter of most supermarkets, may be used instead of the miniature variety.
▲ Serve waffles with melted chocolate and whipped cream.

GREEK YOGHURT, HONEY AND NUTS

A mouthwatering Greek dessert – healthy and simple too

750 ml (1¼ pints) thick full-cream Greek yoghurt
about 60 ml (4 tbsp) honey
about 60 ml (4 tbsp) chopped nuts
sesame biscuits and/or fruit for serving
SERVES 4

Spoon yoghurt into 4 bowls. Drizzle honey liberally over yoghurt and top with nuts. Chill well before serving.

COOK'S NOTES

▲ Chopped hazelnuts, pecan nuts, almonds or peanuts may be used. Alternatively, for an authentic Greek touch, use pistachio nuts. The nuts should be fresh.

▲ Instead of nuts, you can use crushed peanut brittle or home-made praline as a topping.

▲ For a more substantial dessert, stir chopped soft fresh fruit of your choice into the yoghurt.

▲ Thick and creamy Greek yoghurt is available at most large supermarkets. If you prefer, use low-fat yoghurt instead.

APRICOTS AND FIGS IN LIQUEUR

A beautiful, jewel-like dessert that can be prepared in under 10 minutes

125 ml (4 fl oz) freshly squeezed orange juice
juice of 1½ lemons
60 ml (4 tbsp) orange liqueur
about 16 dried apricots
8 preserved figs, with syrup reserved
60 ml (4 tbsp) preserved ginger, with syrup reserved
SERVES 4

Heat orange juice, lemon juice and liqueur together in a saucepan. Add apricots just before boiling point is reached. Once boiling, add figs. Cook for 3 – 5 minutes. Remove fruit and arrange on individual plates. Add about 30 ml (2 tbsp) each ginger and fig syrups to the juice mixture and heat through. Pour over fruit, stud with pieces of ginger and serve on its own or with cream, natural yoghurt or a mixture of both.

COOK'S NOTES

▲ Fresh figs may be used instead of preserved, but then you will need to add a little sugar or honey, or the syrup from preserved figs, to the fruit juices before boiling them.

▲ For a totally different taste, serve a wedge of crumbly blue cheese with the fruit instead of cream or yoghurt.

PEARS SANGRIA

An updated version of the classic pears poached in red wine

- 250 ml (8 fl oz) dry red wine
- 125 ml (4 fl oz) orange juice
- 100 – 125 g (3½ – 4 oz) sugar
- rind of ½ orange
- rind of ½ lemon
- 1 cinnamon stick
- 5 ml (1 tsp) vanilla essence
- 2 cloves (optional)
- 4 firm, ripe pears, peeled, retaining stems

SERVES 4

Bring all ingredients, except pears, to the boil. Reduce heat. Add pears and a little water to cover, if necessary. Simmer until tender but not too soft, about 15 minutes, turning occasionally. Place pears and syrup in a pretty bowl and chill before serving with cream or ice cream.

COOK'S NOTES

▲ This dish is traditionally served cold and may be prepared up to 2 days in advance. This is not a hard and fast rule, however – hot pears are equally delicious. Serve whole, halved or quartered.

▲ Peaches, plums or nectarines may be used instead of pears, but have different cooking times. Plums and nectarines will need 7 – 10 minutes; peaches (depending on the variety) will need 7 – 15 minutes.

DRIED FRUIT COMPOTE

If you've only ever thought of this as a breakfast dish, think again. Add a dash of your favourite liqueur, a few nuts and you have a marvellous dessert

250 g (9 oz) mixed dried fruit
30 ml (2 tbsp) seedless raisins
rind of ½ lemon
15 – 30 ml (1 – 2 tbsp) honey or sugar, to taste
juice of 1 large orange or nut liqueur (Amaretto)
45 g (1½ oz) slivered almonds
SERVES 4

Place fruit in a saucepan and add cold water – to about 2 cm deep. Cook until soft but not mushy, about 15 minutes. Add remaining ingredients, except almonds, and stir to blend. When fruit has cooled slightly, add almonds. Serve warm or at room temperature with cream, natural yoghurt or custard.

COOK'S NOTES

▲ The dried fruit is also wonderful cooked in a half and half mixture of fruit juice and water. If you do this, do not add sugar but rather offer a bowl of honey as an accompaniment.

▲ Use brandy, port or marsala wine instead of liqueur.

INDEX